W H A T   P E O P L E   A R E   S A Y I N G . . .

When I read the first draft of just a few chapters of Carol Frank's new book **Do as I Say, Not as I Did!: Gaining Wisdom in Business through the Mistakes of Highly Successful People** I found I could not put it down. Having lived as an entrepreneur for over forty years I found that Ms. Frank was right on the money. This new book is a "must read" for all new entrepreneurs. Nothing is better for a teacher than experience, and this book gives you lessons from the people who have built and lost and rebuilt business after business. Everyone who is either considering going into business or is already a full-fledged entrepreneur will be able to learn many valuable life lessons from the entrepreneurs who have been chosen to tell you their story so that you may benefit from their successes and avoid the mistakes they made. Reading this book will be an excellent investment of your time.

■ *Peter H. Thomas, Chairman of the Board of Trustees,*
The Young Entrepreneurs' Organization; founder, Century 21 of Canada

"Provocative yet entertaining, funny but insightful, Ms. Frank gets to the heart of what really matters to the entrepreneur—avoiding adversity and maintaining a path to profitability. Entrepreneurs, CEOs, and employees alike will find great take-home value in these compelling war stories."

■ *Dr. Tom Hill, Founder, The Eagle Institute;*
co-author "Chicken Soup for the Entrepreneurial Soul"

"This book contains a wealth of information for the aspiring or practicing entrepreneur. Carol has captured the reality of entrepreneurship with her style of writing about new and emerging ventures. The insight that persistence overcomes adversity is one of the hallmarks of this book."

■ *Jerry F. White, Director*
Caruth Institute for Entrepreneurship
Cox School of Business
Southern Methodist University

In developing The Cooper Aerobics Center over the past three decades, I have certainly made mistakes which nearly led to bankruptcy. Therefore, I can closely identify with many of the entrepreneurs mentioned in this book. I have also learned that being personally and professionally disciplined in both the periods of prosperity as well as periods of near financial failure is the key to success.

One thing I have learned, as have the other entrepreneurs mentioned in this book, is that "Success is certainly more of a journey that it is a destination." Or, expressed another way, "Excellence is not a place at which we arrive so much as it is the means of getting there."

■ *Kenneth H. Cooper, M.D., M.P.H.*
Chairman and Chief Executive Office
The Cooper Aerobics Center

DO AS I SAY
NOT AS I DID!

DO AS I SAY
NOT AS I DID!

*GAINING WISDOM IN BUSINESS THROUGH
THE MISTAKES OF HIGHLY SUCCESSFUL PEOPLE*

CAROL FRANK, MBA

BROWN BOOKS PUBLISHING GROUP
DALLAS, TEXAS

Manufactured in the United States of America.

For information, please contact:
Brown Books Publishing Group
16200 North Dallas Parkway, Suite 170
Dallas, Texas 75248
www.brownbooks.com
972-381-0009

ISBN 0-9760492-0-1
LCCN 2004110054
2 3 4 5 6 7 8 9 10

DEDICATION

I would like to dedicate this book to my
mother, Virginia Rock, who instilled in me
my entrepreneurial spirit.

CONTENTS

*Name has been changed

F O R E W O R D

It was the last pity party I ever had," exclaimed entrepreneur Bill Cawley. His story and the twenty-nine others that Carol Frank shares will end any entrepreneur's personal pity party. And these stories will save you a bundle of money and headaches if you heed the lessons learned. The entrepreneurs in the following pages earned some of the most expensive and practical MBAs on the planet.

For the past thirteen years, I've chaired the MIT/Inc./YEO "Birthing of Giants" executive program held on the campus of MIT. The most popular evening of the program is the Dr. Ed Roberts Night of the Living Dead event. Named in honor of the legendary master of entrepreneurship in the MIT Sloan School of Business, it's an evening in which sixty chosen business leaders lay down their facades and share their most horrifying moments in business—and how they survived.

What's amazing, yet almost comforting, is that these successful entrepreneurs "lived" to tell their stories. Carol's book brilliantly replicates this amazing evening and teaches all of us that the most important value we must hold as entrepreneurs is to never, ever, ever give up. Yes, we might have to change strategies and entire industries, but to persevere as an entrepreneur is in many ways the real test of an entrepreneur.

And the stories, especially Carol's, keep reminding me of a favorite Steve Jobs quote, a quote from the quintessential survivor himself who built a multibillion dollar business before age thirty, only to see his baby, Apple Computer, ripped from his arms. Undaunted, he built another great company, Pixar, and ultimately ended up rescuing his first child. I couldn't help but think that *Finding Nemo* was a perfect metaphor for Jobs's own journey of making his way back to Apple. To paraphrase Steve: "It's amazing how overnight successes take a helluva long time!"

Persevere, learn, and enjoy the journey.

VERNE HARNISH
FOUNDER, YOUNG ENTREPRENEURS' ORGANIZATION
AUTHOR OF *MASTERING THE ROCKEFELLER HABITS: WHAT YOU MUST DO TO INCREASE THE VALUE OF YOUR FAST-GROWTH FIRM*
CEO, GAZELLES, INC.
MAY 2004

PREFACE

One of the most revealing things I ever heard from a professional speaker was that lectures on overcoming mistakes, adversity, and failures invariably outsell others. Some might say it's a dirty little touch of our car-wreck mentality, but I'd like to think it's something nobler. Learning from your own mistakes is experience. Learning from the mistakes of others is wisdom.

At the time I heard this revelation, I was in the middle of fighting the most difficult business battle of my life.

The next revelation set the first in concrete. I was reading a *Wall Street Journal* article entitled "For Motivational Speakers, Nothing Succeeds Like Failure." The article described the hottest new breed of speakers—people whose tales include failure, lessons of recovery, and fighting back. Bestselling business-book author Tom Peters was quoted as saying, "Only with failure can you verify wrong ways of doing things and discard those practices that hinder success."

The final step that led to the genesis of this book came during a conversation I was having with Young Entrepreneurs' Organization's (YEO) strategic alliance/press manager Matt Mladenka. I was telling him about the difficulties I was having with my business and what it was taking to overcome the mistakes I had made. He astonished me by telling me he encountered stories like mine on a regular basis from fellow YEO members. He went on to say that the stories were so interesting and compelling, he thought someone should write a book about them.

Cue the cartoon light bulb over my head.

I had been keeping a detailed journal of the trials and tribulations of my long journey into near-bankruptcy. What's a good journal if not the foundation for a good book? Thus, *Do as I Say, Not as I Did!: Gaining Wisdom in Business through the Mistakes of Highly Successful People* was born. The purpose of this book is to provide entertaining stories about some amazing, successful entrepreneurs who have made mistakes or faced adversity and, one way or another, triumphed by fighting the good fight.

The people included in this book had more than their share of sleepless nights and stress-filled days. My hope is that you can learn from the mistakes they made and the troubles they faced, so that you can gain wisdom, rather than the scars of experience. If you're planning on running a business, you're going to face your own share of troubles as it is—the lessons herein will help you avoid some of the ones others have made.

I hope you take many things from this book and that the dozens of specific examples will stimulate you to take immediate action for use in your own life. I also hope you take away pearls of wisdom that you can pass along to others. But, above all, I hope you breathe a big sigh of relief and say, "Whew, I'm glad it was them, and not me. Now I know better!"

And I wish you success.

CAROL FRANK
DALLAS, TEXAS
CAROL@CAROLFRANK.COM

ACKNOWLEDGMENTS

Writing a book is truly a group effort—to say this book is by "Carol Frank" is an oversimplification. First and foremost, I would like to thank Trey Garrison, my writing collaborator, and the person responsible for many of the laughs in this book.

I'd also like to thank Mark Gluck, a friend and business partner, who assisted me by offering his insight and moral support; and my business mentor, John Roberts, who donated countless hours to help me rebuild my business.

Next I'd like to thank Matt Mladenka, YEO communications manager, for helping launch the project and referring me to many of the people featured in this book; Milli Brown of Brown Books for her wisdom, guidance, and overall professionalism; Lynore Martinez, M.D., for being the best friend, mentor, and book critic a girl could ever have; and finally, all of the entrepreneurs in this book for being willing to bare their souls so that others will never have to.

CAROL FRANK

Carol Frank's Story

NAME: CAROL FRANK

COMPANY: AVIAN ADVENTURES

INDUSTRY: PET PRODUCTS

ANNUAL REVENUES: $2.1 MILLION

I am the master of my fate; I am the captain of my soul.
■ *W. E. Henley ("Invictus")*

Freedom. Freedom is the heart and essence of entrepreneurship. Freedom to captain your own destiny. Freedom to take your business in whatever direction you determine. The freedom brought by financial success and security. The freedom of spirit in seeing your vision realized.

There will come a time when big opportunities will be presented to you,
and you've got to be in a position to take advantage of them.
■ *Sam Walton, founder of Wal-Mart, Inc.*

But what is freedom? Placed in the crucible of life and with all its superficialities burned away, freedom comes down to one essence: options. Having options is both what freedom is and what freedom brings and, ironically, is the means by which freedom is secured.

Entrepreneurs identify opportunities, large or small, that no one else has noticed. Good entrepreneurs also have the ability to apply that creativity—they can effectively marshal resources to a single end. But they have to have the freedom of options to make it happen.

> The successful person makes a habit of
> doing what the failing person doesn't.
> ■ *Thomas Edison*

Entrepreneurs have drive, a fervent belief in their ability to change the way things are done, and the force of will and the passion to achieve success. They have a focus on creating value; they want to do things better, faster, cheaper. And they take risks—breaking rules, cutting across accepted boundaries, and going against the conventional. All because they value freedom as both a means and an end. Entrepreneurs face daily challenges that test both will and resolve, yet they overcome, learn, and grow as they continue on their path.

The entrepreneur's life is just that—a life. As in life, nothing you do can completely prepare you for what you face when you take on the daunting task of being the owner and president of your own company. While there may be support, you're ultimately on your own—your money, time, and energy are personally on the line. But having freedom—the freedom to say no, the freedom to take this path rather than that, the freedom to find your own market, niche, or value—that's what it is all about, and it can make all the difference in the world.

My story is a testament to the importance of having options, freedom, and self-reliance.

My independent streak was forged by a combination of events in my childhood. My parents' divorce and the tragic deaths of both my father and my older brother all while I was young cruelly stole away any childhood notions of permanence and security. Yet despite this and subsequent experiences, I've striven to keep an irresistible optimism and belief in the goodness of life and people.

> Optimism is the faith that leads to achievement.
> Nothing can be done without hope and confidence.
> ■ *Helen Keller*

A former CPA with a master's degree in business administration, I had always considered myself business savvy. My natural demeanor was to look for the best in people, trust them when they gave me their word, and try not to rock the boat by being too hard-nosed.

As an auditor for a large CPA firm, I found it interesting to see how our different client companies worked, and it served as a good basis to expand my understanding of company operations. But I had to get out. After a short stint selling radio advertising and then working as an executive recruiter, I had had enough. Since my teens, I had been setting my own rules, so being stifled by the corporate blanket just wasn't going to work. Although I was going to school at night, captaining two soccer teams, and working as a recruiter during the day, I still found time to come up with a business plan for myself.

The first business I started was an outgrowth of my graduate school project. With help from my boss at the executive recruiting firm, The Animal Kingdom was born. This was before the days of Petco and Petsmart, and I envisioned a large, professionally operated pet store—the anti-"mom and pop." Our plan called for The Animal Kingdom to become a regional chain in time. Although it never grew past a one-store operation, it gave me two new tastes—one of ownership, which was like manna from heaven, and the second, of being an entrepreneurial mind trying to manage retail-level employees, which was not so appealing. In its first year, the business generated almost $800,000 in revenue. It also nearly sent me to the nut house.

I expected round pegs to fit in round holes and square pegs to fit in square holes. Instead I got chaos on a daily basis! The mentality of the people working for me was something I was totally unprepared for. It was a challenge just to get them to show up for work, much less show up on time. One of the people I had managing the store, I found out, was taking the phone numbers of attractive women customers from their checks and bothering them at home. Another was pulling tricks with the cash register, pocketing a couple hundred dollars a week. I spent more time policing the books and dealing with personnel than I did running the business.

CAROL'S VERY FIRST LESSON:

Remember the Chinese proverb—"If you neglect your art for one day, it will neglect you for two." Keep your mind on your money, because no one is going to care about your business like you do. Also, I learned the importance of knowing your strengths and weaknesses. Are your personality and style right for your business?

Despite wanting to get out of the retail end of business, the silver lining was my discovery of what has become a lifelong love affair with exotic birds. I fed and nurtured literally hundreds of baby parrots, and what began as work became a devotion. In

1991, after selling The Animal Kingdom, my parrot passion led to my next venture, a wholesale distribution company specializing in bird products: Avian Kingdom Supply.

Within four years, Avian Kingdom Supply, which had started in a 600-square-foot closet behind the pet store, had grown into a 17,000-square-foot warehouse with twelve employees and $1.7 million in revenues. The main reason for this kind of growth was something most people wouldn't think to build a business around—large birdcages. With the pet bird market still in its infancy (but on its way to the seventeen million birds living in the United States today), there was virtually nothing to choose from if you wanted to house your $1,000 feathered friend in something you would enjoy having in your living room. Wherever I could find attractive cages, I bought them, and they sold amazingly well at solid margins.

In seeking suppliers, in 1993 I found one in Tijuana, Mexico. The company offered a decent product at a reasonable price. Once I picked up their line of cages and started marketing them to my growing customer base of pet and exotic bird shops, the cages sold like antacids at a chili-eating contest. Avian Kingdom Supply was bringing in the cages by the truckload, yet demand continued to outpace supply.

I had found a unique opportunity. Very often entrepreneurs spend much of their lives wracking their brains trying to think of the *Next Big Thing*. Here was a product where the manufacturer could not keep up with demand, and that dynamic showed no evidence of abatement. Smart egg I can be sometimes, a light bulb went off in my head. That year, Avian Adventures was hatched.

First things first. It wasn't enough to just import existing cages from Mexico. All it would take was someone else coming along with deeper pockets or a better distribution network to put Avian Adventures out of business before it could even spread its wings. I wanted something I could call my own. After the *Dallas Morning News* did a story on the success of Avian Kingdom, I got a call from Randall*, who claimed that his family had nine manufacturing facilities south of the border and that he would love to talk to me about being my new cage connection. Randall and his son lived in Dallas, and when they came to visit, they dazzled me with credentials, accomplishments and even a picture of Randall with former President Bush.

They came across as honest and trustworthy, and they offered to make a birdcage for me that looked like the ones I was buying in Tijuana, but for less money. The son claimed to be an architect who would spend several months at one of their factories overseeing the production of the cages.

Unfortunately, the first shipment arrived a few months late and the quality was horrible at best. Within a few days after the shipment's arrival, Randall and son were pestering me to place another order—but this time at much higher prices. I was not pleased with the first shipment so I decided to hold off doing anything for the time being. It's a good thing I did, because several days after the shipment arrived, I received a fax from someone named Carlos* in Guadalajara. My eyes widened as I read Carlos's awkward English. Basically, he wrote that he no longer wanted to sell the cages through a middleman (Randall and son) and asked if I would consider buying them directly from him. My confusion turned to anger as I realized I had been duped—Randall no more had family with factories than I did! Not only had he lied about that, but also it turned out that most of Randall and his son's credentials were bogus.

LESSON:

Don't take promises at face value without doing thorough research on a potential vendor, even one that claims he knows an ex-President.

A core belief of every successful entrepreneur should be, "If you can't do it better or different than your competitor, than you are wasting your time." So I called a close friend, Joel Hamilton, who had a master's degree in landscape architecture and years of experience as Supervisor of Birds at the Dallas Zoo.

"I want something unique," I told Joel, "something that will not be confused with my competitors' cages—a cage on which we will be proud to put the name Avian Adventures."

Joel set pen to paper and in no time came up with several signature designs. Meanwhile, I went to work finding someone who could manufacture the signature Avian Adventure cages, and I found that someone in Mexico. His name was George*, and he had been producing furniture and satellite dishes. He was exceptionally eager to partner with me on this venture, and the enthusiasm on both sides of the border was tangible.

Although I'd learned my lesson about employees, my eternal sense of optimism meant that I assumed anyone working with me as a partner and peer would have the same goals, loyalties, and standards as I. The only reservation I had was logistical: could George produce the first order quickly and up to specifications?

Meanwhile, I had already laid the groundwork for distribution in the United States. A serial networker and natural leader, I was the First Vice President of the Board of Directors of the

Pet Industry Distributors Association (PIDA). I leveraged that position to establish a network of contacts with the largest pet supply distributors in the United States.

LESSON:

Especially in the start-up phases, leading a new business venture can be all consuming, and the idea of taking leadership roles in associations can be overwhelming. Don't fall for this. The more people you know, the more your business grows. I served for PIDA before I started Avian Adventures, and it paid dividends later.

The response to my designer birdcage was phenomenal. By August 1996, Avian Adventures had orders in house for over one thousand cages with no end in sight. Because I was still running Avian Kingdom Supply, I was burning the candle at both ends. It was a relief to me that George and I were developing a solid, friendly relationship, because it was unfathomable to me that a friend and vested business partner could let me down. I even found time to attend his twenty-fifth wedding anniversary celebration in Mexico.

Business grew, and so did the need for a signed contract. In a way, it became all the more awkward because we had become friends. I tried negotiating a contract several times, but George had acquired additional partners to provide capital to grow his business, and they wanted to play hardball with this American gringa. They came back with some extremely unreasonable requests of my company, such as no warranty period, no responsibility to replace defective parts, and the right to reproduce the cage anywhere they wanted with no consequences.

At this point I did what I had rarely done in life—I took the path of least resistance. Business was going well, and I figured that international contracts would be difficult to enforce outside of the U.S. anyway, so I didn't press the issue. Based on that established relationship and on my happiness with my success thus far, I placed my business's future on those two imposters called *hope* and *assumption*.

In June 1997, I invited George to be my guest at the pet industry's largest trade show. Although things were going well, there were some minor complaints from customers about details of the cages and the packaging. So it just made sense to me; rather than constantly relaying these concerns to George, why not let him hear it from the horses' mouths? I thought it would impress upon him the need to fix the problems.

During the trade show, I pointed out the booth of a much larger competitor. I explained to George that the company had asked me earlier that year if they could buy Avian Adventure cages for resale. Since I was barely keeping up with the demands of existing customers, I declined, and I was even more adamant about it when I later heard from reliable sources that the company was going to outsource their own manufacturing to Mexico in an attempt to put me out of business. I went on to tell George how important it was to keep up the quantity and quality of our product since we were going to have this new competitor vying for our cage business.

Sometime during that fateful weekend, George walked into the competitor's booth and introduced himself to the owner with an oily smile and a cold-blooded handshake. "I make cages for Avian Adventures and I would like to make them for you."

Jesus was betrayed with a kiss; I didn't even get that courtesy.

A BIRD IN THE HAND AND A KNIFE IN THE BACK

This clandestine backstabbing began to unfold over the next several months. By July 1997, Avian Adventures was on track to do $2.5 million in sales for the year. Customers were waiting upwards of eight weeks for their shipments because of the backlog created by the success of the product. Then, in the middle of a particularly crazy and seemingly prosperous summer morning, George called and said, "Carol, we will no longer ship you any product unless you pay us up front."

"WHAT?" I exclaimed. "Are you kidding? We have over $100,000 in orders ready to ship! I've been paying you within fifteen days. What are you going to do with my cages if I can't come up with the money?"

Unfortunately, the answer came soon thereafter.

LESSON:

You can't get away without a contract no matter how many wedding anniversaries you've attended. My mistake was ordering even one cage without an agreement that would prevent George from making birdcages for anyone else using my design. My second mistake was not getting a patent for my design that would, at least, be valid in the United States.

It only got worse from there. In October 1997, one of my best customers, Mike, called. He said, "Carol, I just got a call from one of your largest competitors. They offered to sell me Avian Adventure cages."

"No way!" I replied. "They must have offered you cages similar to Avian Adventure cages." Because no one could be that stupid, underhanded, or ballsy, I thought to myself.

"I'm afraid not," Mike answered. "They told me that they had made a deal with your manufacturer to buy your cages."

Each word felt like a slap in the face punctuated by a punch to the gut. I had transformed George, a small-time satellite dish maker, into a multimillion-dollar birdcage manufacturer. And this was his idea of saying gracias. But my anger at George's betrayal was tempered by the anger I felt toward myself. My intellectual capital had been stolen, and I could have prevented it!

I had put so much trust in George and was so busy running both Avian Adventures and Avian Kingdom Supply that I hadn't bothered to spend the time or money to patent my cage design. On the brink of tears, I telephoned an intellectual property lawyer only to find out that since the cage had been on the market for more than one year, it could no longer be patented.

"Your only option is to get a copyright on your drawings, and that probably won't do you a lot of good," the lawyer offered. I took the advice at face value, got my drawings copyrighted, and took no immediate further action.

Left with the impression that there was nothing I could do about George or my competitor, it seemed painfully obvious that I would have to accept the fact that my much-larger competitor was going to sell my company's design as their cage. Throughout the fall of 1997, my competitor repeatedly contacted almost all of Avian Adventures' customers, trying to steal business. I was saved only because I had forged solid relationships with my customers. I lost only one out of ten customers directly to my competitor.

Through dogged determination and keeping my word to my customers, business continued, but sales topped out at $2.1 million in 1997, 1998 and 1999, and the rapid growth curve flattened out. Unfortunately, I still had to buy from George because, like it or not, he had me over a barrel.

During the four years I bought cages from George, I knew I needed a second source for my product. 'Sourcing, sourcing, and more sourcing' was something my Young Entrepreneurs' Organization's forum members would urge repeatedly. However, it was just so easy buying from one person who really knew what he was doing.

In 1997, soon after "the betrayal," I began an earnest search for a second source. It began with Gerardo, also from Mexico, an automotive parts maker. I did my due diligence—I'd learned from the Randall fiasco—and Gerardo's reference checks came back stellar.

Over the next year and a half, I devoted six trips, hundreds of hours, and over $25,000 to get Gerardo's production of Avian Adventure cages up to speed. His first shipment in June 1998 (which took six months to finish) was a complete disaster. It had gone to one of Avian Adventures' distributor customers in Houston, and Avian ended up taking the entire shipment back.

In hindsight, I should have cut the relationship off immediately after the first bad shipment—his promise to me of making perfect cages right out of the chute was broken. But he was just so nice and I was so eager to make things work with him that I gave him way too many chances to prove himself. Just because someone can make auto parts does not mean he can make birdcages. That I was eager to get a second source and dump George like a bad habit played into it as well.

A "CUSTOMS" SOLUTION

In August 1999, while still buying from George, I began researching having my cages made in China. It was then I discovered that U.S. Customs has a program where they will detain shipments at the border that infringe upon copyrights, trademarks, and patents. For example, if customs discovers a container full of jeans with a "Levi's" logo on them, they will contact Levi Strauss to ensure that the jeans are legitimate. If they are not, then customs agents will seize the shipment. **My original copyright lawyer never told me about this program.**

LESSON:

A common theme throughout this story is the importance of having options. That goes for legal counsel as well. If a doctor told you that you had a terminal condition (which in effect this was for Avian Adventures) you'd get a second opinion. Having only one lawyer means having only one perspective. In all fields, and especially something so malleable as civil law, a second and third opinion and options can mean the difference between life and death for your business.

I immediately registered my copyright with the U.S. Customs Department and flew to their Laredo office to meet with an inspector. I put my hope for justice into the hands of the federal government.

It came in the form of a phone call I received from George in early November of 1999.

"Carol!" George screamed. "What do you think you are doing holding up my shipment at the border?" Oh sweet, sweet revenge. I could hardly control my excitement. I had been waiting for this moment for two years.

"You are going to ruin my business!" He went on to say, "I am not going to ship you another cage until you release the shipment that is being held by customs." At that moment, I didn't care whether I ever sold another birdcage again; I wasn't going to give in to this man and I was already finding new options.

"No," I replied icily. "I will not release that shipment just because you are threatening me. I don't care if you make birdcages for someone else—just don't make them look like mine."

George backed down. He said, "I have a new design that doesn't look like yours, and I can e-mail you a picture of it tonight. If you approve, then perhaps you can release the shipment back to me and I will rework the cage with the new design."

For the first time in over two years, I felt hopeful that the nightmare of having my cages sold by a competitor was coming to an end. Looking at the pictures of the new design, I was ecstatic to see that the cage was sufficiently different from mine and, therefore, people would no longer confuse our cages. I would no longer have to endure the pain of having people approach my booth at trade shows with puzzled looks, saying, "I thought Avian Adventures went out of business." "I thought you were bought out by your competitor." "I thought you couldn't get any more cages because George was selling them all to your competitor."

Some days are better than others. This was one of those days. In an ordinary life that wasn't destined to test the limits of passion and persistence, our story might end here.

In the fall of 1999, The Mexican Trade Commissioner referred me to yet another potential manufacturer, Alex*. I received a beautiful sample from him and that, combined with the fact that his brother-in-law lived in Dallas, gave me enough confidence to not only place an order in December 1999 but to also do something I had never done before—send an advance to Mexico for over $11,000. I was sure I finally had a viable backup to George. But the perils of not having a proven backup manufacturer were about to hit home.

LA CAGE AUX FOLLES: THE LAWSUIT

Convinced that I had won a major battle against George in the "war of the birdcages," I forged ahead with my improved 'Cage 2000' design, a third-generation model that my staff and I were most excited about. This cage was really going to set me apart from my competitor, especially now that they had to change the look of their cage. Unfortunately, on January 13, 2000, one month after sending Alex his first order, an event transpired that almost sent Avian Adventures the way of the Dodo bird.

A process server from the Dallas County Sheriff's office walked into my office and served Avian Adventures, Inc., and me personally, with a lawsuit naming us as defendants. My competitor was suing me for Fraud, Deceptive and Unfair Trade Practices, and Unfair Competition.

"What?" I asked incredulously. "Why in the world would *they* be suing *me?*"

Furiously flipping the pages of the thick document, I found my answer in Exhibit A, an affidavit signed in October 1999 by George, three days after his shipment was detained at the border.

The affidavit, which is as legally binding as if the signer were under oath in court, stated that George was making birdcages before I met him in 1995, and that he was the sole author and original designer of the birdcages named in my copyright.

The suit read: "As part of an unlawful scheme to disrupt my client's business, AVIAN and FRANK filed a fraudulent application with the U.S. Copyright Office to register the copyright in the Work. In this application, AVIAN and FRANK intentionally made false, deceptive, and misleading statements of material fact so that the Copyright Office would rely upon them to issue an invalid copyright registration. These statements at least include FRANK's statements that I am the author of the Work and AVIAN's statements that it is the owner of the copyright when both AVIAN and FRANK knew that MANUFACTURER was the author and owner of the copyright in the Work."

George claimed in a subsequent phone call, during which I was imagining all manner of sadistic tortures, that he didn't know what he was signing (even though he has an MBA from Tulane and speaks fluent English), and that he was fully aware that he was not the original designer of the Avian Adventures cage, only that he had made some improvements in the way it went together.

I speculated that because George lived outside of the U.S., he felt he was immune to a perjury charge, and he signed this document to keep his other customer happy. After four years and millions of dollars in business, I stopped buying from him that day. I placed a call to Alex and asked him if he was ready to take over all of my business. Of course he eagerly said yes, and I pulled all of my business from George and gave it to John.

Fortunately, I still had nearly every bit of correspondence I ever had with George, not to mention Joel's original drawings with dates and signatures. I wasn't worried about losing the suit; I was worried about how I was going to pay for it.

LESSON:

Keep all documents relating to communications with suppliers and customers. Be familiar with your insurance policy coverage, and when in doubt, ask.

The fourth lawyer I consulted on the matter (I was all about second and third opinions now) told me to submit this lawsuit to my insurance company and ask to have it covered under my Business Liability policy. Sure enough, they reluctantly came back with an agreement to handle the suit "with reservation." "With reservation" gave them the option of going to court to have a judge determine whether Avian was entitled to coverage, and subsequently the insurance company filed a lawsuit against Avian asking the court to determine who has responsibility to pay for the suit. Fortunately Avian prevailed, because the suit ended up lasting two and a half years and cost over $250,000 in legal fees.

In the meantime, I had to try to keep Avian Adventures alive. During February and March 2000, I sent Alex orders for eight hundred cages totaling over $150,000. During one of my many visits to his factory he looked me straight in the eye and said, "Carol, do not worry. I guarantee there will be no problem having one thousand cages made by the end of March." One of the reasons why business had heated up so much was because I had taken the beautiful sample that Alex had made for me to a few trade shows. I had begun promoting our new improved 'Cage 2000' to my customers and the orders were pouring in.

The first ship date came . . . and went, with assurances from Alex that the next date would be no problem. The second ship date came . . . and also went. After the third missed ship date, I began to worry that I had made an enormous mistake. It was April 19 and my customers were wondering where their product was. I had gone full force promoting this new product and they were getting impatient waiting for it.

LESSON:

Always under promise and over deliver.

Not having product for two months would wreak havoc on anyone's cash flow. To make matters worse, I had fallen for Alex's sob story that he had to have $70,000 to start production since my order quantity had increased so much. Normally, I would never send money to a manufacturer until I have finished product, but I felt backed into a corner because I had already cut off George.

I asked Alex repeatedly to send back some of my money. "I am going to get a bank loan and send you back some of your money shortly," he constantly insisted. No such bank loan ever materialized, and I later discovered that Alex's modus operandi was to ask for advances on new projects so he could pay off old debts. I had fallen into the same trap as I had with Randall. I failed to do enough due diligence and as a result, fell victim to a slew of empty promises. In hindsight, I should have asked to talk with at least three of his recent customers to determine their level of satisfaction. I also should have talked to his banker and demanded to see his financial statements before sending any money to him.

LESSON:

You can't over check. There is no such thing as too much due diligence.

It just got worse from there.

It was the end of May when sixty cages finally left Alex's factory.

Without my approval, Alex had decided to save money by contracting with an inferior paint company (I had given the green light to a different company) and the paint was flaking off in our customer's hands. Compounding the problem, he had purchased recycled single-ply cardboard boxes in which to ship 75–120 pound metal cages. Not only did UPS destroy almost every cage, but they also refused to pay for the damage, claiming that they had been improperly packaged. In fairness to UPS, they were correct. Avian Adventures had to refund thousands of dollars to unhappy customers.

In August, Alex finally scrapped the rest of the poorly-painted pieces and started new production. At the beginning of September (nine months after I had given him my first order), he had some new cages to take to an approved powder coating facility, Tecno Alambre. He called me the first week of September to tell me that three hundred cages would be painted by September 15 and on their way to Dallas by the

19th. Having already pre sold most of this shipment, and desperate to keep my business from going under, I arrived in Mexico on September 27 to inspect the entire shipment (already a week late).

The first situation I encountered was that no cages had been painted. Weeks later, it was discovered that the cup holders did not fit into the cages. Finally, I told Alex I was sending a truck to pick up whatever cages he had ready. I just had to have some product. Not only was my company running on fumes, my reputation was in shambles.

On November 28, 147 cages arrived in Dallas. The good news? Customers loved these cages and not one was returned. I had always had faith that the design, features, and colors of my cages far surpassed my competitors'. I knew if I could just get them made, I could get them sold. But the extreme delays started to take their toll on my distributor customers. Avian Adventures had been the exclusive provider of birdcages to the United States' largest group of pet supply distributors. But by the end of 2000, all of them had jumped ship in favor of my competitor. My sales plummeted from $2.1 million to $300,000.

INCOMPETENCE NORTH OF THE BORDER

When I realized Alex was in over his head, I knew it was time to try something completely different. I contacted an old friend, a seasoned and insightful local business executive, for some advice. He introduced me to an enthusiastic gentleman, David*, who had a highly-automated machine shop eight miles away from our offices. My friend felt that if anyone could make these cages for me in the United States, David could.

In June 2000, David and I reached an agreement for birdcages that cost only 5 percent more than I was paying in Mexico. I was ecstatic. In an effort to keep Avian Adventures' customers from jumping ship, David wrote a letter to them insisting he could have seventy-five to one hundred cages per day by mid-August. His letter emphasized how he specialized in high volume products and that this one would be no exception.

You know what happened next. By the end of August, David had not produced a single cage. His excuse was that some of his employees had quit, and he was having a hard time hiring new ones, and the product was more difficult to make than he had anticipated. In mid-September, David informed me that his investors were pulling the plug and that he was closing up shop. He would have a total of fifty cages ready by early October and that would be all. I began thinking that perhaps divine providence had decided to treat me like my birds do the bottom of a birdcage.

I contacted three other machine shops in the Dallas area to see if they could make the cages, but all of their bids were significantly higher than what I was paying in Mexico. Frustration led to despair as I realized how disappointed my customers were going to be that the MADE IN THE USA cages were not going to be.

In the meantime, I was still involved in the lawsuit with George.

IT AIN'T OVER TILL THE BIRDCAGE LADY SINGS

In what clearly started out as a ploy by my competitor to "squash Avian Adventures like a bug" and put me out of business, the tide eventually turned in Avian's and my favor. As part of my defense (and thus paid for by the insurance company), Avian counter sued both the competitor and George for copyright infringement—something I had wanted to do for many years but for which I had been unwilling to spend the money or endure the emotional heartache.

Two and a half years and 30,000 documents after it started, the judge in the lawsuit strongly encouraged both parties to settle and avoid going to trial. In August 2002, the case was settled and I walked away with enough money to pay off my short-term debt and resuscitate the ailing Avian Adventures.

The timing was fortuitous because Avian had completely run out of cash after exhausting every resource available. I had tried a total of fifteen manufacturers for my precious product. Friends, family, and business acquaintances kept telling me to throw in the towel. But, I was PASSIONATE about my feathered friends, I just couldn't give up on my dream of making my livelihood through helping better the lives of companion parrots. I had just located an acceptable manufacturer in China and the first order was getting ready to ship. Finally, I was going to have product to put Avian Adventures back on top, and I needed the settlement money to get there.

This new manufacturer did not disappoint. In 2003, Avian Adventures had the most profitable year in the history of the company. Today the company is back on track to exceed its highest level of sales, and I have a new perspective on everything from life to business.

Like many people, I was cocky enough to think that I had my business all figured out. I was armed with a CPA, MBA, and years of experience! Little did I know that I would end up earning my PhD in the Philosophy of Life.

From having been through a legal and business nightmare where I didn't know, literally, if the next month I might be bankrupt and homeless, I achieved a sense of Zen balance in my life. My business is still my passion, but I take time out to enjoy other aspects of my life as well.

I am no longer hesitant or timid about making people meet my expectations. In my heart I am still the eternal optimist, and I hope for the best from people, but you're going to sign a contract if you want to do business with me, and you're going to live up to my expectations. With the battle scars of courtrooms proudly on my sleeves, I am not afraid to use every resource I have to make you keep your end of the deal. "Deeds, not words" has been etched into that faculty of my mind that evaluates people.

And above all else, in every aspect of my life, I seek the freedom of having options. I simply will not be tied down to one offer, one consultant, one expert, one lawyer, one manufacturer, one realtor, or one anything. (I may make an exception for my romantic life, but not just yet.) Why? Because more than the financial success, and more than the legacy building, and more than passing fancies like acclaim and prestige, I value my freedom. That's why I went into business in the first place.

And even when I lost, I didn't lose the lessons.

> "Far better it is to dare mighty things, to win glorious triumphs, even though checkered by failure, than to take rank with those poor spirits who know neither victory nor defeat."
> ■ *Theodore Roosevelt*

> "Only those who dare, truly live."
> ■ *Ruth Freedman*

*Names have been changed

Section One

Know the Business You're In

AMILYA ANTONETTI

NAME: AMILYA ANTONETTI

COMPANY: SOAPWORKS

INDUSTRY: NON-TOXIC CLEANING PRODUCTS

ANNUAL REVENUES: NOT AVAILABLE

Amilya's Soapworks makes natural soap-based household cleaners for those who suffer from allergies, asthma, and chemical sensitivities. They are hypoallergenic, non-toxic, biodegradable, cruelty-free, and made from the highest quality pure vegetable oils. All clean superbly and make human- and earth-friendly cleaning easy, effective, and affordable.

A few years ago, Amilya's newborn son was having severe problems. David's first years were mysteriously filled with nonstop screaming, breathing difficulties, and rashes. Traditional medicine didn't help, so a desperate Amilya turned to homeopathic and alternative doctors for help. She discovered David's hysterics and difficulties were an allergic reaction to the chemicals in everyday cleaning products. The household cleaners from the grocery store shelves were loaded with toxic chemicals. When she tried natural cleaners, David did not react adversely to them, but they were expensive and hard to find, and they did not clean very well.

Amilya started making her own natural soap products. When she shared her cleaners with friends and neighbors, word spread like wildfire. That was when she decided to start her own company.

The problem was, while she had experience in owning businesses, she didn't approach this new venture strictly as a business—she was out to help people—so she didn't give much thought to learning how the industry she was in worked. Amilya sold all her assets to get the company up and running, and only after she was fully committed did something occur to her.

She would have competition. And it would be the likes of Dial, Clorox, and Procter & Gamble. Now, David may have slain Goliath, but the reason that story stands out in people's memories is because things like that don't often happen.

Amilya realized she had chosen an industry that is the definition of branding and marketing. They don't call them soap operas for nothing. Commercial television got its very start in the 1950s through sponsorship by the major household cleaning products companies. Her major competitors were billion-dollar companies with advertising and marketing budgets running into tens of millions.

"They spend millions and millions to get people to know their product," Amilya said, recalling her panic. "How the heck can I?"

Furthermore, in what she admits was pure naiveté, she never bothered to research exactly how the grocery industry works. She just assumed, as so many outsiders do, that grocery stores and drugstores are always on the lookout for the best products for their consumers.

"I didn't realize it was a 'real estate' business—that every square inch of shelf space costs money, and it goes to the top bidder," she said. "So I realized I was up against billion-dollar companies that could spend millions on branding. Well, I had sold everything I had to put into this company of mine, so failure was just not an option."

Amilya knew what would make or break her was branding and public relations. She had to brand the company name, and she had to educate corporate buyers about the advantages of her product over the big soapmakers. But she didn't know how to go about doing it.

"So I just went and got the biggest and best PR company out there, and I paid them a bunch of money," she said. "And I got absolutely nothing on my investment. They didn't do a thing. I was too small a client in their huge stable, even though their fees were bleeding me dry. I didn't even pay myself during this period, yet I got nothing from them."

Amilya withdrew her association with the big PR company, and sought a new one more in line with both her company's size and her way of thinking. Through cost-effective marketing, consumer and corporate education, and not just a few guerrilla marketing tactics, she began establishing brand awareness and getting her product on store shelves. Today her company is a nationwide success, and her products are found in grocery stores, drugstores, and health supply stores.

LOST:

Amilya estimates that she lost several years in cashflow growth because of the financial burden she imposed on herself by hiring a huge public relations company, and in time lost when that company did not accomplish any of her goals.

WHAT HAPPENED:

JUST WHO ARE YOU UP AGAINST?

Amilya went into the soap business like a cliff diver—head first and at near-terminal velocity. Passion was her driver, as it is with so many successful entrepreneurs. But it can't be an entrepreneur's only asset. The cliché is that knowledge is power—well, it's a cliché because it's true. She didn't bother to learn who her competitors were. She didn't try to learn beforehand how grocery stores stock their items. She didn't think through what it would take to build a brand name. Instinct is good, but it will only get you so far. As a result of her lack of due diligence, many of her moves that should have been proactive were reactive, on the fly, or badly chosen. She admits that had she not sunk everything she had into Soapworks, she might have completely pulled out from panic when she realized she was up against "The Big Boys" of cleaning products.

THE SHOE DIDN'T FIT.

Going after the biggest and best name out there—be it a public relations firm, law firm, accounting firm, or whatever kind of vendor or service provider—is not necessary, especially in the early stages of a company's life.

"I went for too big, too fast," she said.

Smaller firms may not have all the resources of the bigger players, but the smaller service provider may be more the partner a new company needs. A smaller advertising agency will be as anxious to partner with a new company as the entrepreneur is to have a partner in that area. Such an agency will answer their own phones and they will take a more proprietary interest in the entrepreneur's success. They see it as making an investment.

"You can't wait for decisions or responses from big companies when you are moving at entrepreneur speed," Amilya said. "If I call a lawyer and he doesn't get back to me in forty-eight hours—heck, in forty-eight hours, I could remake the world. It's overkill. You don't need that. You need someone who is really going to work for you."

QUESTION:

Have you analyzed the strengths and weaknesses of your competition before launching a new product? Do you have the capital to sustain a retaliation attack by them?

Are you choosing the right-sized service firm for your organization, or are you under the erroneous assumption that bigger is always better?

MICHAEL BEROLZHEIMER

Venture capitalist Michael Berolzheimer has a passion for consumer products. He's been involved in the successful development of items that are national household names, and he heads up the first venture capital company, Early Stages, specifically and solely focused on consumer products.

With a Harvard MBA and a unique background in wood product development (he is behind the development of the labor- and frustration-saving DuraFlame™ log), Michael had experience that spans more than just two continents. It is a model lesson for anyone in business. The scenario itself—a western company trying to break into a unique eastern market—may not appear to apply to just any business. But when you look closely, you'll see that it's really a lesson that could apply to trying to make a trade across the street, or even across cultures.

There's an almost Rashomon* quality to the story of this one gaijin's** attempt to earn a share of the chopstick market in Japan.

PROBLEMS CAN ARISE, CHOP-CHOP

"I always liked to be a big fish in a small pond, from athletics in prep school to running a fraternity. I like to have a large share of a small market, and that's why I saw an opportunity in the Japanese chopstick business," Michael said.

Michael, along with his brother, was running P&M Cedar Products, a sawmill business, at the time they spotted what they thought was a remarkable opportunity. Having had extensive experience in developing wood-form consumer products—both in specialty woods and in the development of the now ubiquitous DuraFlame™ log—Michael figured he was highly suited to exploit this opportunity.

Michael had discovered that the supply of wood for a certain kind of chopstick was under threat. Specifically, the issue was chopsticks made of alder—an item in high demand in Japan. Alder is found in Japan but the supply is dwindling. The tree is also found in Canada, so the idea Michael had was to set up a business to harvest, process, and deliver alder chopsticks to Japan from British Columbia.

Michael and his brother found a site north of Vancouver, Docile Creek, and armed with a business plan, $3 million in outside capital and $2 million of their own funding, ginned up operations marketing chopsticks.

The concept was simple: Michael's company would form a partnership with Louisiana Pacific, which was in the processing business of manufacturing oriented strand board. "We would take the highest quality logs—all Louisiana Pacific wanted was fiber. We would take the very best logs to an adjacent factory to process into chopsticks," Michael said.

Their advisor on style and quality, a Japanese national whom they hired as their salesperson, provided the specifications, and the company went to work.

"After a year and a half, we ran into many problems, but we gradually got the plant operating. After four years, we wound up producing a million to a million-and-a-half chopsticks per day," Michael said.

So what could be the problem?

"We thought we understood the definition of chopstick quality. We had hired someone in Japan who had spent time in the chopstick industry to be our salesman, so we thought he knew the nuances and details. But the facts are that after we got the initial product into the marketplace, we got feedback saying the quality was not satisfactory. We did nineteen things to modify the quality. And it still wasn't right," Michael said.

But a chopstick is a chopstick, right? Wrong. Michael learned that in Japan, the very quality of a restaurant is measured by the kind of chopsticks used. There are the basic chopsticks—most often found in the equivalent of fast-food restaurants in Japan and in most Asian restaurants in the United States—called koban. They have no bevel and are made simply and quickly. (Think the Japanese equivalent of the plastic "spork" you get at KFC.)

Then there is the kenroku, reserved for more upscale restaurants. The Japanese place great scrutiny on this style—they must be made of white wood, have beveled edges, have no knots, and symmetry and even planes are critical. The highest-grade chopsticks, kensoga, are as carefully selected at upper-crust restaurants in Japan as cuts of filet or a style of fine crystal are at an American five-star restaurant.

"What we found out was the fellow we had hired in Japan either did not know what the quality standards were, or, if he did know, wasn't able to communicate them, or he wasn't listened to, or he didn't want to be assertive in correcting our mistakes," Michael said. "Our containers, at this point, were in Japan and being rejected by wholesalers.

"We didn't understand the quality of the product or the demands of the consumers," Michael said. "There were other mistakes we made in the process, but above all we didn't understand what it was the customers were demanding."

LOST:

About $6 million.

WHAT HAPPENED:

EVERYONE IS A GAIJIN SOMEWHERE.

The Japanese have a unique word for foreigner—gaijin, meaning literally, "barbarian." On reflection, Michael realizes that his product fit that description—it was improper and crude to its intended market niche. His company didn't understand the subtleties of consumer tastes, owed in this case to a cultural divide and/or miscommunication.

"From the president on down, to be successful, a company has to understand the nuances and details of a product and what a consumer wants from it," Michael says. "I should have spent weeks learning specifically the varying differences in each level of quality, and specifically what they meant to Japanese people and the Japanese restaurant business, long before we drew up the first page of specifications for our product."

Such a divide is easy to see in hindsight, crossing two cultures as it does, but there are equally great divides within a culture or a market. Why does this stuffed pink teddy bear with a rainbow on its belly become the hottest holiday seller, while a stuffed pink teddy with a cloud on its belly languishes on the shelves? Why do these kinds of pants fly off the shelves while retailers can't give away an almost identical style? When you're an outsider to a market such as Michael was, seeing and understanding the differences and nuances can be difficult.

It's not enough to know what the product is that you want to sell. You have to know why the consumer wants it. You have to know what that product means to them, far beyond its functionality, and even far beyond its image.

BLINDSIDED

A few years later, Michael was involved in another cross-continental wood product manufacturing enterprise. The idea: manufacture Venetian blinds from the abundant basswood supplies in China using cost-saving Chinese labor, and import the products to the United States.

"We'd learned our lesson, we thought. We took the time to study the logistics and the reality and the product. After a lengthy study and business plan, we entered the basswood business. It took two years to study the business. We studied the quality of the product, having learned from past mistakes. We put together the funds. It was a three- to four-year process. We got the plant started and we had one customer. We shipped three or four test containers," Michael said matter-of-factly. "That's when the first problem appeared."

The initial problem, actually, was that Michael started with one customer instead of the three his business plan called for. Turns out the blind manufacturing and wholesaling business are rife with politics, where exclusivity is the norm rather than the exception. But that wasn't a huge problem.

The subsequent challenge with that first shipment showed that there was a sorting and quality inspection problem. Again, nothing Michael wasn't prepared for. This is a standard start-up business problem. Michael improved the inspections, increased the number of quality inspectors, and even improved the lighting for the inspectors.

This work done, the plant fired up production. Even though there was a slowdown of orders from their initial client, the plant still carried on with production in an effort to build up a good-sized inventory. They basically had faith the orders would come. When they got their next order and delivered it, there was a new problem.

Michael ended up taking a seminar to learn this particular industry nuance. In order to look for flaws, people in the blind business will hold a slat up in a certain way to a certain kind of light. Unfortunately, a flaw was seen in his company's production of slats that was unacceptable in the blind business. "I was sure we had studied every detail, but this one was new to me," Michael said sheepishly. "So now we had three problems—an inventory that was no good, a flaw in our product, and a flaw in our production. Meanwhile, cash is going out and going out."

Michael and his team scrambled to fix the production problem, but it took more than nine months to set things right. His client held on to him because Michael had built a solid relationship, but in the end several factors ended up bleeding the venture of all capital until, well . . . curtains.

LOST:

Several years and $4 million.

WHAT HAPPENED:

SAME AS BEFORE, DESPITE HAVING LEARNED THE RIGHT LESSONS.

Michael is no dummy. He didn't go into this . . . ahem . . . blindly. He did his due diligence to the best of his ability. He learned his lessons from his chopstick fiasco. He studied this venture for several years.

The problem is, there are always going to be unknowns. You have to be prepared for the fact that your plan may not survive contact with reality, and that you may have to move faster than you've ever moved to correct your course. Michael did his best but a myriad of factors conspired against him, and that could happen to anyone. But his refusal to accept anything but full responsibility, and his total embracing of the lessons learned the hard way, speak more highly of his character than even his many business successes could.

"It was a quality issue in the enterprise. We thought we knew quality, but we didn't know it to the nth degree necessary," Michael says. "We could have saved ourselves had we had in place from the beginning a process for understanding and meeting the quality requirements of the customers. Make sure you have it right; then make an extra investment to make sure you are sure you have it right."

QUESTION:

Are you sure you have met and exceeded your client/customer expectations?

Really, really sure?

If so, maybe you should check again. Confidence can be a killer, and nothing is wrong with checking under the hood one more time.

Rashomon is a stunning collection of short stories by Ryunosuke Akutagawa and considered a masterpiece of modern Japanese literature. The collection includes the short story "In A Grove," which recounts through varying and differing eyewitness accounts the events surrounding a highway robbery in feudal Japan, illustrating how people invariably see the same events differently, or hear the same words and take different meanings from them.

**Gaijin: The Japanese term for a non-Japanese, literally translated as "barbarian."*

GARY HOOVER

NAME: GARY HOOVER

COMPANIES: BOOKSTOP, TRAVELFEST

INDUSTRY: RETAIL BOOKSTORE CHAIN/
RETAIL TRAVEL STORE

ANNUAL REVENUES: $65 MILLION/$25 MILLION

Gary Hoover is the archetypal entrepreneur—he moves fast, he has had as many failures as successes, his eye is always on the horizon, and he doesn't know the meaning of the word quit. He has made, lost, and made again millions; he's had the rug pulled out from under him by everything from a board of directors to an industry paradigm shift. Yet he is undaunted in pursuit of his vision, and he's often changed the way business is done. Been to a book super-store lately? He pioneered the concept. Used an Internet-based information service? He helped pioneer the concept.

First and foremost, Gary's passion is the retail business. He enjoys imagining new ways to bring products and services directly to the consumer and serving the diversity of his con-sumer base. Gary's first company, started in the 1980s, was BOOKSTOP, which, by the time it was sold in 1989 to Barnes & Noble for $41.5 million, had become the fourth-largest retail book chain in the country. What happened to him in 1987, after bringing in new venture capital (VC) partners, was a preview of a lesson he would learn later. The BOOKSTOP board, at the behest of the new VC partners, wanted to bring in an experienced CEO to helm the company, which they felt had outgrown its initial entrepreneurial growth stage. Because of the power they wielded, the VC partners were able to oust Gary with little warning and little in the way of transition.

"It hurt me personally, and more important, it hurt the company," Gary said. "I had to appeal to a lot of the other executives there not to jump ship when I left. I wanted the company to continue and succeed after having built it up over the previous seven years. That was my first experience with putting too much control over what I was doing in one group's hands."

Gary's next company was The Reference Press, which was later renamed Hoovers. Hoovers provided general company information and background on all public and many private companies. Hoovers.com became a research mainstay for everyone from investors to job hunters, and from business analysts to business reporters.

"As an entrepreneur, I realized that there was a lot you have to learn about an industry you're going into, and then I realized that most business people don't know much about business," Gary said. "They tend to believe myths. They don't know much about their industry from the outside. Most people don't know jack about a company they are interviewing for or investing in. And that's a need that Hoovers met."

Hoovers was sold to Dunn & Bradstreet in 2003 for $117 million. That idea worked better than Gary had hoped. But it was his third company idea that brought him his biggest life lessons: Travel Fest. Seems like such a happy name, but when all was said and done, it would become a business nightmare for Gary Hoover.

The idea, born in the early 1990s, was to create a giant travel superstore, marrying travel agent service with specialty travel product sales and solutions. Travel Fest carried luggage, maps, and books. It provided full travel agent service. Customers could exchange currency at the day's rates for the coin of whatever realm to which they were going. The store would even have in-house language classes for pleasure or business travelers. And while most travel agencies were only open the standard 9 AM to 5 PM, Monday through Friday, Travel Fest was open seven days and late into the night, both to serve store customers in person and to assist clients no matter where they traveled.

Gary couldn't get VC money—the more innovative a concept is, the less likely venture capitalists will be interested. So he turned to angel investors, as he had when he started BOOKSTOP, and he also raised capital through a self-underwritten stock offering under State of Texas laws.

In all, he raised $13 million, which enabled him to open three stores between 1994 and 1997. Two stores were in Austin and one was in Houston. The reception? Far beyond Gary's best expectations.

"We thought we'd do about $1 million a year per store in books and luggage, and we did about $800,000 per store, and that's at a 35–40 percent gross margin. We missed a little, but we were in the ballpark on those sales," Gary said. "It was airline ticket sales that blew us away.

"We thought that after the first two or three years to get established, we'd get up to $3 million in sales per store, and then the commission was about 10 percent," Gary said. "But man, the travel agency side opened the first year at about $10 million in sales per store. It just popped like crazy. All of a sudden it was the major part of the business. We had to scramble to get experienced travel agents in there."

Things were going great. And that, of course, is when the other shoe fell.

In late 1997 and early 1998, the major airlines sought to cut costs, and one of the first methods on the table was to slash the commissions paid to travel agents. That commission had become a major part of Travel Fest's cash flow.

"And that's exactly when we didn't need our cash flow hampered," Gary said.

Gary scrambled to find creative ways to make up the loss. Traveler fees were considered, and he beefed up book and luggage sales, since they held a higher profit margin. Change, scramble, be creative—words he lived by in the aftermath of the airline cuts. He franchised the idea out to other travel agencies. Expanded into the idea of kiosks at malls and airports.

When things got tight, Gary wouldn't give up. He took out a $300,000 home equity loan; he borrowed hundreds of thousands from friends to put into the company. He had to expand to stay afloat, and he started looking to institutional investors.

"I'd go to their offices and see two newspapers on their desks—one with the headlines about how the Internet was killing travel agents, and the other about how airlines were continuing to cut commissions," he said. "So it was a no-go."

He sold one of the Austin stores to a local travel agency, but it was just a delaying action in what became a full-scale withdrawal from the battlefield. Despite a valiant fight, Travel Fest eventually went down. With it he lost a large portion of the money he'd made with BOOKSTOP and Hoovers, and he walked away with a lot of debt.

But Gary remained the fighter he always had been, and he is now working on creating a new business—a fourth new start—and at the time of this writing, he will only say it's a retail business dealing with nostalgia and history. He knows the lesson that some of the greatest entrepreneurs and names who became household synonyms for success often only won after years of struggle and setback.

"The risk is real. It's not just something you read about in a textbook," Gary said. "There's a reason entrepreneurs are rewarded. The chance they take can swallow up their whole life."

LOST:

More money than Gary Hoover would care to remember—his own and that of his investors. And for a short time, his confidence as an entrepreneur.

WHAT HAPPENED:

NOT DIGGING DEEP ENOUGH ABOUT THE INDUSTRY HE WAS ENTERING.

It's ironic, Gary admits, since one of the companies he'd started had been Hoovers, which was designed to provide more information to business people about businesses and industries. But though he spent a lot of time researching the travel business and even meeting with airline executives from two airlines, he really had no idea that most of the airlines hated travel agencies. He was blindsided when the airlines started cutting travel agency commissions.

"The main reason for failure was a change in the industry, and I didn't see it coming."

You cannot ever know too much.

ALL THOSE PRECIOUS EGGS, AND HE ONLY BROUGHT ONE BASKET.

There are those who can make it work, but Gary realized with his experience with Travel Fest why he prefers retail—it provides the broadest range of market potentialities, a.k.a. the individual consumer.

"I don't want to be reliant on any one thing. With retail, while you want to satisfy every customer, if they just don't like the way you do business or aren't happy, that one customer is 1/100th of 1 percent of your business."

Gary went into a business where his fate was in the hands of one kind of supplier: the airlines. And such an industry is almost lockstep in business practice—as one airline goes, so goes the lion's share of them.

"A primary objective of being an entrepreneur is achieving your vision and controlling your own destiny. When you're reliant on one type of supplier, one type of vendor, one type of customer, or even reliant on government policy, you are powerless if there's a shift. I never want to be in a position where suppliers, customers, or regulators have their hand on my faucet."

He even learned that lesson in a different manner with BOOKSTOP—the second round of venture capitalists who invested in 1987 suddenly had control over Gary's destiny—and they ousted him with little ceremony or consideration.

Today, Gary has just published his own book, *Hoover's Vision: Original Thinking for Business Success.* The book is all about what it takes to succeed in business—especially the big picture and strategy. It is also his vision of what the future can hold for individuals, society, and America, if they look within to what can be rather than looking outside with a cynical vision of what cannot work.

QUESTION:

If you are searching for outside money to fund growth, have you "looked your money in the eye" to find out exactly why your investors are interested in your company? The answer may not coincide with your long-term goals.

Have you interviewed the company founders of some of the other companies in their portfolios to determine whether they are satisfied with the arrangement?

Is your major source of revenue subject to government regulation? If so, are you actively pursuing ways to diversify?

DORTHY MILLER

NAME: DORTHY MILLER

CURRENT COMPANY: THE MILLER AGENCY

INDUSTRY: ADVERTISING AGENCY
SPECIALIZING IN AUTOMOBILE DEALERS

ANNUAL REVENUES: $12.5 MILLION

Dorthy Miller's story brings to mind the lyrics from the classic Gary Neuman song from the 1980s:

"Here in my car, I feel safest of all, I can lock all my doors, it's the only way to live. In cars."

Dorthy knows automobile marketing like the best mechanics know auto repair. More than twenty-five years ago, she was a buyer for a department store and teaching marketing and merchandising at a junior college in Lexington, Kentucky. An auto dealer who knew her work in other fields asked her to come aboard and set up an in-house advertising agency for his dealerships.

Dorthy threw herself into it with a passion, and soon there wasn't much about automotive sales that she didn't understand. She knew what sold and what didn't. She knew how to entice buyers, how to plot long-term strategies, and the ins and outs of everything from design and media buys to what was important to dealers.

A few years later, Dorthy was hired away by an advertising agency—then known as Maxina Agency—and within three years, she bought out the owner. Thus, The Miller Agency was born. By 1984, she moved the company from Lexington to Dallas, where today the firm has more than $15 million in annual billings and is a premier advertising company for auto dealerships in Texas, Oklahoma, and Arkansas.

Today, she is confident that if she and her team can get the meeting with the right decision maker, there's no client in the auto dealership world she can't land. But it wasn't always a smooth ride, and she's had to work to make sure all eight cylinders were firing and the engine stroking smoothly.

For starters, Dorthy never meant to become such a niche market expert, and she's tried several times to expand beyond the automobile sales industry. And while she knew she was an expert in one part of the industry, she never realized that there were other elements of marketing automobile sales that she didn't quite grasp either.

It happened about two years after buying Maxina Agency and renaming it The Miller Agency. A salesman for a company approached her and her clients, selling a syndicated automotive campaign—print, radio, and television materials, all bundled and ready to roll out. The price for each campaign was $10,000. It was, in Dorthy's estimation, a campaign that probably cost about $10,000 in total to produce—and then she saw that they had sold the same campaign to about sixty other dealerships in different markets.

It got Dorthy's wheels turning.

"You do the math. It wasn't even that great a campaign, and I thought that I could do a much better job," she said. "So, since I knew so much about the industry, I just jumped in without looking."

Dorthy assembled a team to put together a much better syndication package. The production cost alone was $20,000. She hired a team of salespeople and sent them out on the road.

"And we did absolutely zero in sales," she said, matter-of-factly. "So I brought in a new team of salespeople and sent them out on the road."

Still, the engine wouldn't turn over. Time for a product tune-up?

"I thought, *I am stubborn. I will make this work.* I kept hammering away, and produced a newer, even better package of syndicated materials," Dorthy said.

She spent another $40,000 on a new package. And still nothing, or the next thing to it. There were a few sales here and there. Unbundled, some dealers were willing to buy the radio and newspaper advertising components, which ran much, much cheaper than television advertising.

"I just kept going and going, driving on, and I never saw the real problem," she said. "So I took my hard-earned money plus money I didn't have, and I lost it all."

Dorthy recovered. Despite the insistence of her accountant, she did not file bankruptcy—she had too much pride and honor. She put herself to work. She cut expenses, including payroll, and worked herself harder than ever. She made her agency lean and mean. Within two years, she erased her debt and started to build again.

Today, almost two decades later, The Miller Agency is an industry leader specializing in auto dealerships. It employs twelve experts who get done the work of many more than a dozen. Reenergized from a recent sabbatical, Dorthy and her crew are planning on expanding beyond The Miller Agency's traditional geographic boundaries. And she's doing it with the confidence of an expert who knows there's no limit to what she can accomplish, so long as she knows what she is doing, where she is going, and that what you don't know can hurt you.

LOST:

Almost a quarter million dollars, in 1983 dollars.

WHAT HAPPENED:

DRIVING WITH BLINDERS ON GETS YOU BLIND-SIDED.

Dorthy never thought about anything beyond the fact she knew she could produce a better product. She did not consider other factors like the fact that producing syndication packages for auto dealerships was all that other company had ever done. They had a large, established client base.

"And I was new to the whole thing outside of Lexington. No one had a reason to go with what I could offer them," she said.

Another big factor in her scenario was the state of the economy. At about the time the ad agency selling the packaged ad campaign came through Lexington, the national economy was going gangbusters. Dealerships were flush with money and would buy the syndication package even if they never planned to use it.

"They'd pay $10,000 at the time just to take it off the market," she said. "I didn't factor in that the economy was changing, and that dealerships wouldn't be so casual with their spending."

Dorthy only focused on one part of the whole—the product. She knew she could make a better product, and she was right. But product alone doesn't mean much if you don't take into account the myriad other factors that shape the marketplace. A man named Preston Tucker once created the most advanced automobile of its time—incorporating quality, comfort, engine, and safety features decades ahead of its time. His company never made it off the ground.

Bottom line—always, always, always do your due diligence. There is no substitute for market knowledge and you can never have too much.

"In retrospect I should have gone to them and said, 'I can see you're selling this like crazy, but we can improve your product', and approach it from that angle," she said.

TOO MUCH IN-HOUSE CAN PUT YOU IN THE POORHOUSE.

There's no need in this day and age to keep everything under one roof. Dorthy learned early and the hard way that if you keep your employee base low, you can improve your profit margin while still getting the work done.

"We now do a lot more than what twelve people can do. I got my overhead out of whack with all those people, particularly all the salespeople I hired for the syndication project," she said.

Keep your staff lean. Learn the importance of contract assignments.

KNOW WHAT YOU KNOW, AND DO WHAT YOU KNOW.

Be an expert at something. Know the field you are in. There's always a market for someone who is at the top of that particular field.

"I see a lot of TV and radio ad reps who see how much money auto dealerships spend, and they jump out and try to start their own agencies, but they don't know the industry and they end up on their face," she said. "And if you can't do it better or differently than your competitor, you may as well not bother."

QUESTION:

Do you know what markets you want to sell to? Are you sure they will need your product or services?

Are you considering expanding your product or service offering? Have you determined with 100 percent confidence that you can do it better or differently than your competition?

WILLIAM "BILL" CAWLEY

NAME: WILLIAM "BILL" CAWLEY

COMPANY: CAWLEY INTERNATIONAL

INDUSTRY: COMMERCIAL REAL ESTATE

ANNUAL REVENUES: $25 MILLION

I've made tons of mistakes," Bill Cawley says, with an easy smile.

With an opening statement like that—coming from a man who has built a virtual empire in commercial real estate services, development, and telecommunications, with annual revenues around $25 million—there's hope for every entrepreneur. Aside from having built six million square feet of commercial properties and providing corporate real estate services to companies nationwide, he is the leading retailer for Cingular Wireless in five states, having grown to more than ninety stores from a dead start a couple years ago.

In fact, Bill's life story is a testament to facing obstacles and overcoming them—be they of his own making or an act of unfortunate Providence. The man has literally had misfortunes that he shouldn't have survived. More on that later; first, a little about how he started building his company and some of his early missteps.

After his divorce, Bill took a getaway trip to Dallas in 1982 and found a real estate guy's nirvana. "Buildings were being built on every corner," he said. "I had a passion to be in a bigger market and wanted to earn a name for myself apart from my father. I thought, *What better place than Dallas?*"

He did great for a while, but then the commercial real estate market took a nosedive. After the Dallas real estate market crashed in the mid-1980s, Bill went to work for the Bass brothers in Fort Worth. "I didn't enjoy it because what I was doing was calling on my peers who were in trouble, taking their last dollar off the table," he says.

Undaunted by the market conditions and tired of what he was doing, a year later Bill launched his own firm, Cawley & Associates, which he ran from a bedroom in his house. Business was slow. It took six months to save enough to buy a fax machine.

"I had a plan. I realized that people used to make decisions in real estate on a local basis in the 1980s. If they had a real estate need, the manager of that office would handle that locally," he said.

As technology developed for companies to track costs more closely, they started seeing they had no focus on real estate cost. So around that time, companies started making decisions on real estate more centrally, at the corporate level.

"I started calling on Fortune 100 companies. I flew up to see anyone who would see me and talked to them about handling all their real estate. I learned that they'll see you, but they won't do business with you if your company is too small," Bill said.

For twelve months he traveled, calling on big companies, and didn't get a dime's worth of business.

In desperation, he turned to local start-ups and smaller companies.

"These were companies that, when I called on them, had three employees—CEO, CFO, and secretary. No one was calling on them, so they wanted to do business with me," Bill said.

Bill would provide them with whatever corporate real estate services they needed, from simple lease negotiations, to cost analysis, to site selection.

Sometimes it would take a while for the relationships he built to become truly profitable. But as these start-ups grew in the late 1980s and early 1990s, he grew with them. The relationship had been forged.

"We went from doing zero business to millions in revenue in the course of four or five years," he said.

LOST:

A year's time, opportunities with the right clients, and lots of travel money.

"It got to the point where I was living off friends. As broke as you can be. I even had my gas meter pulled."

WHAT HAPPENED:

SOMETIMES YOU HAVE TO TAKE SMALL BITES.

Bill was right about how real estate needs were evolving. He was right that he could provide the services the Fortune 100s needed. He was right about everything but the fact that often, large companies don't have much faith in smaller companies to provide services.

"I was right about everything but who my proper target was, so I spent a year chasing rabbits," he says. "Big companies will talk to you even though they have no intention of doing business with you because they have people who are paid to talk to you anyway."

FINDING HIMSELF—AT THE BOTTOM OF A RAVINE

By 1996, as the height of the 1990s real estate boom in Texas was approaching, Bill faced a setback that was of his own making, but it taught him his most valuable lesson in business—and life.

Bill was in Colorado on July 5, 1996, zipping down a two-lane road near Aspen on his new motorcycle. He tried to pass a car and a dangerous game of chicken ensued. Cawley hit the brakes to avoid an oncoming car and was catapulted over a thirty-foot cliff at sixty miles an hour. The impact crushed both of his arms and his right leg. His head, held together by his helmet, felt like it was in a bucket.

"It was an accident I shouldn't have survived."

"I believed in my heart that I was taking my last breath," Bill said. "Everything that seemed important to me before then—all the leases I hadn't signed, all the deals I hadn't done—didn't matter anymore. My family, my children, and the legacy I was leaving behind as a person all became incredibly important.

"Then I began to think about God," he says. "I realized if I died, I wasn't sure where I was going to go."

About twenty minutes later, Cawley heard the voices of his two riding buddies on the road above him. Realizing he had a chance to survive, he used his one good leg to thrash his way up the hill and collapsed at the top. He was flown to a hospital where he went into surgery—for nineteen hours.

The next morning, a male nurse used a piece of rubber to stick a spoon in Bill's bandaged fist, trying to get his patient to eat some cereal.

"I was just starting to realize how bad things really were, and I started crying," said Bill, who was forty-three at the time. "The nurse put me in a wheelchair and took me outside to get some fresh air. He sat me under a tree and left me there. It happened to be next to the entrance where paraplegics get dropped off for their daily therapy.

"For four hours, I watched people struggle to get out of their vehicles and into the building," Bill said. "It was the last pity party I ever had."

The real estate broker's yearlong recovery involved nine surgeries. He spent most of the time in bed. He couldn't brush his teeth or bathe himself. He needed help to go to the bathroom. During those twelve months, as Bill was flat on his back, his company went horizontal too. Bill had always had his hand in everything at his company, but without him, others in the company stepped up to help lead things. The full-service real estate firm was transformed from a vertical organization into a flatter one.

In the process, by letting go of his need to control every aspect, he and his company began to flourish.

LOST:

Iron-fisted control of his company.

WHAT HAPPENED:

PLAYING CHICKEN ON A MOTORCYCLE IS NOT A GOOD IDEA

He remembers lying in the hospital bed thinking he was going to go broke. But everyone really stepped up. The people he thought he always needed to direct knew their jobs, and he had invested them with a sense of ownership in what they did.

"It made me realize I didn't have to be involved in every little detail. In fact, my company did extremely well without me. It was a humbling experience, but it was also a very rewarding experience," Bill says. "I learned to delegate because I had to, and when you have the right people to delegate to, it works better than anything."

Bill took it steps beyond that. He learned to put people in roles where they only had to do what they liked to do and what they were good at. He didn't have to be the rainmaker as he was before. He didn't have to carry the weight of the world on his shoulders if he had the right people.

"I put in place ways to find out what people's strengths are. Most people don't even know what their own strengths are. We test people to determine it. We don't base a whole lot on interviews because the best interviewees may have call hesitation or other issues. Some people's greatest strengths are job interviews. References are good, but don't put too much stock in them. Too many companies are just passing around their old junk. They either want to be rid of someone with no hassles, or they are fearful of lawsuits."

Part of Bill's process in finding new talent is to find people who are successful in other industries besides real estate, but who have a focus in sales. He finds the ones who have the skill sets he needs and who are in a job where there is a ceiling on their earnings.

"The negative is you have to feed that employee longer and it's longer before they become productive, but when they do, they are happier and they are loyal. I've brought in people making $200,000 a year, and within a year or two they were making $2 million," Bill says.

LET'S GO FOR A RIDE

None of Bill's other life lessons are as dramatic as that, nor are they as life-changing, but they are wise words for the entrepreneur seeking equity partners.

Bill got burned on a money deal a few years before his accident.

It was the mid-1990s when the economy was just getting good again. He had secured a development site but didn't have enough money to close on it. He went looking for money partners and found two potential ones.

One company had a great reputation and track record but was difficult to deal with. They weren't giving Bill a very big piece of the opportunity, and the cost of the money was high. (In real estate development deals like this one, the equity partner takes his portion first, and then splits the remainder of a profit with the developer.)

The other company negotiated until the eleventh hour but offered Bill a bigger upside, with one caveat attached—they wanted the right to terminate the developer without cause. Bill—keep in mind this is before his motorcycle accident, so he laughs that he can't blame it on the blow to the head he took—chose to go with the one offering the bigger upside. And the watchful reader will have seen a nearly universal theme—he didn't do any real background checking on the equity partner.

"It was a better money deal, and I didn't expect anyone would do what they did," Bill said. "They let us educate them and start the project, and then they terminated us."

LOST:

About $2 million.

WHAT HAPPENED:

CHECK BACKGROUNDS. CHECK BACKGROUNDS. CHECK BACKGROUNDS.

"I went for money instead of the right relationship. If I had checked them out with people in town, I would have found out they'd screwed other people over before," Bill says.

There was even an early telltale sign. At their third meeting over dinner, this equity person—who was married—brought to the dinner as his guest his girlfriend.

"If you're going to cheat on your life partner, you're going to cheat other people," Bill says. "I should have known."

As a closing note, not only did Bill recover from all his obstacles financially, he's also back in fighting shape and has full use of his legs and hands again.

In rebuilding his company and his body, he also rebuilt relationships with his son, who now works at his company, and his daughter. He met and married his second wife, Keely, and traded in his motorcycle for a convertible.

He also developed a deep spiritual relationship with God, which he says now guides the way he runs his business.

QUESTION:

How well do you know the market you're targeting? Is your company in the right position with respect to size, capital, and product offering to effectively tackle that market?

Are you choosing between several potential joint-venture partners? Do they conduct themselves in a way, both personally and professionally, that would make you proud to be associated with them?

Section Two

Employees: A Necessary Evil?

MICHELLE LEMMONS-POSCENTE

NAME: MICHELLE LEMMONS-POSCENTE

COMPANY: INTERNATIONAL SPEAKERS BUREAU, INC.

INDUSTRY: SPEAKERS BUREAU

ANNUAL REVENUES: $9 MILLION

Michelle Lemmons-Poscente has made many mistakes in building up the highly successful business that is her passion—International Speakers Bureau, a thriving business that connects organizations with leading professional keynote speakers, motivational business speakers, leading executives, entertainers, and athletes for meetings and events.

It's quite typical for successful entrepreneurs to have the notion that other people will do as much and care as much as the entrepreneur does. It's only after things go wrong that many entrepreneurs learn the hard way that this notion is simply false. She also learned the hard way that the more casual approach that entrepreneurs can take when their businesses are small doesn't work when the businesses grow to a certain critical mass.

"Too often I think I've worked from the notion that other people were thinking what I was, and could perform as I would, and that they had the best interest of our common goal in mind," Michelle said. "I've learned that in so many avenues, you have to get it in writing and put in place a clear process."

A case in point—most of her staff at the beginning were referrals from business associates and friends. They were hired on a handshake and casual check of references and nothing more. And that worked, at least when the company was small enough and the staff topped out at ten to fifteen employees.

But even when she started doing background checks and credit histories, problems arose from assuming the best in people.

"Our controller hired this woman as a bookkeeper. She was so good at first that we decided to let her control and handle my personal accounts, including bank accounts that I share with my husband," Michelle said. "From time to time we'd open up our bank statements and see ATM withdrawals—$100 here or $200 there—and we wouldn't think much of it. We each travel a lot and we just assumed it was the other withdrawing the money."

What they didn't know was that the bookkeeper had simply used her access to Michelle's accounts and an online application form to attach a debit card to their personal accounts. And since the bookkeeper was in charge of monitoring their account no one was the wiser.

Fortunately for Michelle, separate issues caused her to have to let the bookkeeper go. Basically, despite being apparently good with the books, she was constantly tardy and called in sick too often. A month later, Michelle's new bookkeeper discovered the discrepancies from Michelle's account, which totaled $7,500. Michelle recovered the money by confronting the former bookkeeper and threatening criminal prosecution. But she learned that you can't let the fox watch the henhouse—you have to be the final reconciler of your own books.

Another case in point—Michelle was looking to take International Speakers Bureau to cyberspace. She needed a Web site as dynamic as her company, which had fully established itself. Like so many entrepreneurs who are a bit single-minded in focus, she didn't know the first thing about how to set one up. She assumed if she found a high-profile consultant, then that person could execute her vision on the Net. Working from a reference from—here it is again—a friend, Michelle hired a consultant, outlined what she wanted, and told him to get to work immediately. No need for a design outline, architecture outline, or even a written contract. Sort of the way an entrepreneur might go with the first recommendation on his or her first facsimile machine when buying supplies for Day One. Fine for a $100 investment, maybe, but for a large undertaking by a successful, growing company . . . ?

Dutifully—and assuming that the consultant was as meticulous about his own business as she is about hers—Michelle paid invoices without question and waited for her Web site, which never really materialized. At least not anywhere near the scope that she had initially envisioned. In fact, even if the consultant had delivered, having learned more about where the Web fit into her overall marketing strategy, Michelle has since concluded that it still wouldn't have been worth the investment.

"I paid $180,000 almost blindly, and even if that person had delivered what I wanted, it would not have been a worthy investment," Michelle said. "We need a Web presence, but as it fits into our overall marketing plan, it is not a major component."

Another mistake was in hiring people on word-of-mouth references alone. Michelle has often assumed more of people than they deliver. Perhaps that is the price of entrepreneurial optimism. It was also the precursor to four knives in the back from four such hires.

Not long after the consultant incident, and well into ISB's stabilization of success, Michelle started putting her energy into a companion business, Mentorium, an innovative online learning concept. It was a good time. Michelle was directing her energies into Mentorium and simultaneously receiving positive profit reports and happy feedback from International Speakers Bureau. One business successful, another one in the planning stages—what could be better? Maybe a few less knives poised at her back.

Michelle was interrupted in her ongoing work on Mentorium one day by a longtime employee, who informed her that he was joining three other ISB employees who were starting up their own business to compete with ISB.

Ever taken a punch to the stomach when you weren't ready? That about covers Michelle's reaction. After she'd picked her jaw up off the floor, she inquired how this all came about. Turns out two of her salesmen and her accountant had become good friends outside of the office. Moreover, they'd decided that they could probably do a better job than ISB was doing, and in part that surmise was informed by the consensus that Michelle no longer cared about ISB anyway, with as much time as she'd been throwing into Mentorium.

It got ugly from there. Michelle had to hire a lawyer, who showed up at the office the next morning with an off-duty police officer. The sight alone caused one of the four Judases, who had an outstanding warrant for an unrelated traffic violation, to literally bolt out the back door and over a fence. The lawsuits got underway, based mainly on the employee agreements they'd signed regarding non-compete and non-disclosure. It then came to light that the four Judases had gone so far as to steal those records from the on-site personnel files.

Although it was a lucky stroke that Michelle had required employee agreements in her start-up days, she didn't have backup copies of the personnel files off-site. She couldn't prove they'd ever signed them. Fortunately, Michelle was able to bring in forensic computer experts who were able to reconstruct deleted files and communications which were incriminating for the four Judases. The four settled out of court, and Michelle absorbed their new company into her own.

Michelle shut down Mentorium. She moved her offices back down onto the sales floor of ISB—a way to run up the flag to her whole company about how committed she was to ISB and its success. A renewed focus on her primary business allowed her to reengineer its approach, allowing it to resume growing.

LOST:

A near revolt, theft of proprietary knowledge, at least $1 million, a woman's jacket with four knife-holes in the back (not really).

WHAT HAPPENED:

FORMAL PROCESSES ALL AROUND. TWO ON MONDAYS.

This can't be said enough, and it seems every entrepreneur has some brush with personnel problems because of this.

HAVE A FORMAL PROCESS IN PLACE WHEN IT COMES TO HIRING.

Even if your partner is a college friend, a war buddy, a sorority sister, a relative—have a formal hiring process, and put the important points in writing. This includes background checks, a formal interview process, criminal checks, credit history checks, and a check with references.

In fact, while the usual situation is for the big corporations to have the formal hiring process and the smaller start-ups to be more casual, that's the exact reverse of the way it should be. Heck, the corporations have the deeper pockets and legal teams for dealing with personnel issues. The entrepreneur doesn't.

Make sure you get non-compete and non-disclosure agreements in writing, and then keep them out of that employee's reach.

STAY INVOLVED.

Stay involved with your employees, or if you've grown beyond the size where you deal with employees on a one-to-one basis, have a process for making sure they know you're involved with the company. Michelle inadvertently became the absentee landlord. It would have been fine for her to devote her energy to developing Mentorium, had she set in place senior proxies who would reflect her own enthusiasm for ISB. Of course the president of GM can't be there every morning to shake each line worker's hand, but the key is to have in place a process of communication, visible involvement with the company, and trusted seniors who can act as proxies for the entrepreneur to instill in those employees that same enthusiasm.

"When we grew from five to ten people, that was manageable. You're used to, as an entrepreneur, touching everyone, being in touch with them. When we grew from fifteen to thirty, you can't touch everyone. That's when you start having to have a process in place.

EVERYTHING NEEDS TO BE IN WRITING.

A handshake is as good as a contract, if you're a cowboy or if there's no money changing hands. In the real world, if something is going to cost your bottom line, get it in ink. That can't be repeated enough. Get it in ink. Michelle essentially wrote a blank check to her Internet consultant, because she got neither the Web design nor the final cost estimate in writing. She also did not outline her expectations or set a limit on what an acceptable cost was.

CHECKS AND BALANCES.

You can't rely on one person to watch your accounts, personal or commercial. You need at least two people handling them, to notice if there are any discrepancies from the other, and you need to check into any withdrawal, debit, or payment you don't personally authorize.

IDENTITY THEFT RIGHT AT HOME.

With the right info, anyone can get into any account you have. A controller or bookkeeper has to have a lot of confidential information and has to be given some degree of trust—but have you checked with your bank to make sure that someone can't come along and attach a debit or credit card to your personal or business accounts?

NEW VENTURE? SET A MAX.

Even if Michelle had gotten everything she wanted out of the Web site she had designed, it wouldn't have been worth $180,000.

"Anytime I undertake a new venture now, I go in with a set ceiling cost, and if I can't get what I want by the time I reach that ceiling, I walk away," Michelle says.

Michelle, like the biblical Job, endured more than her fair share of employees who tried to take advantage of her. And like that character, she grew the better for it. Today her business is prospering more than ever, and you can bet your bottom dollar that she takes a formal approach to everything from personnel to financial audits. She has truly taken to heart the old adage, "Fool me once, shame on you, fool me twice, shame on me."

QUESTION:

Are you checking references—THOROUGHLY—on every employee or key supplier?

Are you requiring salespeople and other key executives to sign a valid non-compete agreement?

MARILYNN MOBLEY

NAME: MARILYNN MOBLEY

COMPANY: ACORN CONSULTING GROUP, INC.

INDUSTRY: PR CONSULTING

ANNUAL REVENUES: NOT AVAILABLE

Marilynn Mobley founded Acorn Consulting Group, Inc., after twenty successful years as a professional communicator. A former journalist and senior media relations manager for IBM, Marilynn built Acorn on the relationship capital she had established in both the corporate and media worlds. She focused her one-woman home-office operation on providing public relations representation for clients. Because of the kind of results she achieved, she soon had more companies asking for her services than she could accommodate.

"I grew tired of telling people 'no,'" Marilynn said. "I thought if I could duplicate myself, I could bring on these new clients and increase profits. I wanted to grow my business beyond the initial position."

Her idea was simple and sound enough on paper—hire someone with an appropriate background, pay a solid salary, avoid the overhead of office space by having him or her work from home, have that person provide the same service to clients Marilynn provided, and bill that person's work out to clients at about three times the employee's annual salary, the standard billing rate/salary ratio in the public relations industry.

Marilynn had just the person in mind. Katie* had served under Marilynn at IBM as an intern, and had gone on to work for the company in communications at the same time Marilynn was there. While Katie did not work directly under Marilynn after the internship, they knew each other and developed a good friendship. Marilynn hired Katie at a starting salary of $60,000, matching her IBM salary, and covered the cost of setting Katie up with a functioning home office as well as additional training seminars and associated expenses.

"The idea was she would provide the service to these new clients who had secured our services based on my name. I knew her assets—she had the knowledge and the skills. What I didn't know about was what she lacked," Marilynn said, "or how that would cost me."

Within six months, the pattern had emerged: Clients were complaining about Katie's lack of response. Plans were not being executed. The absence of discipline was showing through the empty promises and the façade of competence.

Marilynn believed it was a situation that could be handled by giving Katie a full understanding of the consequences of her inaction. She explained the importance—the critical necessity—of client response and of execution to completion. Katie gave Marilynn reassurance that she would bring more discipline to her work.

Weeks dragged on—Katie didn't follow through with that promise either. Marilynn's company began losing money and clients faster than a stockbroker pushing WorldCom. Marilynn stepped into the breach, certain that Katie's lack of performance could be rectified. In doing so, she sacrificed service to her existing clients and thus saw further damage to her reputation. The financial drain was so bad that Marilynn stopped paying herself a salary for four months. Katie never missed a paycheck.

Finally, after one year and numerous attempts to jumpstart her one and only employee, Marilynn realized she had to cut her losses.

"I just couldn't make it work. It was difficult. We'd been friends a long time. I told her I was sorry, but it wasn't working. I told her she hadn't lived up to her end of the deal."

It took hard work, time, and earnest effort, but after cutting Katie loose, Marilynn finally got her company back to its pre-fiasco footing. While it was in itself not a lesson worth the initial cost of her mistake with Katie—she could have learned the lesson without that problem—Marilynn did realize she wanted to recast her business model. As such, by focusing on providing strategy consulting rather than the more time-consuming task of execution, it put her consulting practice on a better tack for revenue growth. Today, her one-person shop serves as strategy consultant for a number of Fortune 500 companies, earning retainers for her services far in excess of her billings as a public relations representative.

And that had been her goal from the start.

LOST:

About $250,000, based on salary, equipment, benefits, training, lost clients, lost opportunities, and time spent repairing damaged business relationships.

WHAT HAPPENED:

EXPECTING SENSE OF OWNERSHIP IN A NON-ENTREPRENEUR.

Some people have the entrepreneurial spirit, some don't. It can be learned and nurtured, but only if the seed exists. Marilynn made it too easy for Katie. She took Katie from her 9-to-5 corporate world—with its safety nets and guaranteed salary—and expected the kind of self-discipline and aggression that enterprising people who work without a net bring to the ring.

"Katie was never hungry. She got her paycheck every two weeks. She didn't know what it was like to go without one. I mistakenly believed when I brought her in that because she was a friend and had worked for me before, that she would care enough about my business to give her best for it. But no one cares about your business as much as you do. She said she cared, but at the end of the day, she got paid whether she worked for it or not."

Had she known, Marilynn would have come up with a more creative, performance-based way to pay Katie to nurture that entrepreneurial spirit.

LETTING FRIENDSHIP INTERFERE WITH JUDGMENT.

Marilynn never bothered to check with Katie's previous managers at IBM. She never asked them point-blank about her performance. She did not demand of Katie what she would have of an unknown. In hindsight, Marilynn believes many at IBM were "mum" because they were glad Katie was leaving.

"She is the kind who needs the direction, management, and anonymity that a big corporation can offer. I like her personally. She just didn't have a work ethic—she had knowledge and skills, but she was just lazy. I didn't let myself see that. I let emotions and friendship override logic."

No matter how small a company, an owner has to treat employees in the same manner a larger company would—dispassionately, objectively, and fairly. Anything less is a disservice to both.

Backgrounds must be checked. This can't be underscored enough. Anyone can learn how to sell himself or herself up front. Entire seminars are devoted to this. Books, too.

In this litigious age, it can often be difficult to get honest employee references. Use a little creativity. One manager of another company Marilynn knows has a unique practice that protects former employers. The manager calls deliberately after hours and leaves a voice mail for the prospective hire's old employer. The manager says that she is considering hiring the person in question, and that if the employer can give the highest recommendation for the employee, then would they please be sure to call back within twenty-four hours of the message. If not, call back after twenty-four hours, or don't call at all.

The manager tells Marilynn it has not failed yet. Employers who respect a former employee will go out of their way to call back within the time window.

References must be checked, and it is never enough to have someone simply say, "I can discipline myself," when he or she has no track record of it. The personality must fit the objective.

GROWING FOR GROWTH'S SAKE.

Not every business model is meant for growth in every way. Garnering more clients/customers or hiring more employees is not the only way to grow revenue.

Growth by duplication cost Marilynn revenue growth. Growth by recasting her practice from representation to strategy consulting expanded her revenue and client base while freeing up more of her time.

THE HUBRIS OF SUCCESS.

Marilynn's success in both the corporate and consulting worlds created a sense of invulnerability in employee management. Even while bleeding money, Marilynn was convinced the situation was tenable, temporary, and repairable.

Not every situation can be fixed as one wants. It is a poor leader who sticks to a plan for the sake of the plan when it is clearly not working. Reevaluation, flexibility, and adaptation to reality are the hallmarks of success.

QUESTION:

Are you contemplating hiring someone you know into a position in which they have little to no previous experience? Have you thoroughly assessed his or her strengths and weaknesses to make sure you are not trying to fit a round peg into a square hole?

Name changed for confidentiality

TIM BARTON

Tim Barton is the kind of entrepreneur who can almost make another entrepreneur transcend positive, constructive envy and go right to outright jealousy. Now, nothing is as simple as it appears, and every "overnight success" is usually years in the making—but Tim has an uncanny track record of going into an industry of which he knows little and turning a small investment into a multimillion-dollar success.

A self-described serial entrepreneur who has been coming up with business ideas since his days running a paper route in Chicago, Tim started his first business, a telecom company, while still a graduate student at LSU. Starting in 1990 with a handful of college friends, between 1990 and 1996 they built the business into a $22-million in revenue company. They took it public and it grew even faster. In 1996—when Tim was thirty—they sold the company for a cool $240 million.

Tim took a couple of months off to do nothing but work on his next big idea. He had the capital to get a new company up and running, and he had the understanding that the transportation industry was still operating at a level not much past the 1950s in terms of communications.

"Basically I heard from a lot of people that the trucking industry was screwed up—all old-fashioned phone calls and faxes," he said. "I had absolutely no experience in trucking. Just with telecom and Internet."

To the brave goes the glory, as they say.

In 1998, he established freightquote.com. The company uses state-of-the-art technology to offer a centralized directory where business-to-business customers can view the offerings of multiple carriers. The site eliminates the delays and the haggling of the auction process by offering real-time instant ratings with aggregated pricing for less-than-truckload, truckload, expedited, local cartage, and intermodal freight.

Once the shipper enrolls, he enters details including origin, destination, weight, and class. The system returns with all the options available and allows carrier selection. The site further simplifies shipping by providing automated freight documents, consolidated weekly billing, and online recordkeeping.

The company now boasts 160 employees. The revenue growth has been phenomenal. In 1999, the company had about $1 million in revenue. In 2000, it jumped to $15.5 million, followed the next year by an increase to $33 million, and in 2002 it breached $60 million.

The thing is, that kind of growth comes at a cost. The cost is the human capital used to take it from one stage to the next, and the emotional toll that comes when you have to cut loose those who helped grow the company along the way—be they partners or employees.

The ugly fact is, Tim says, that at the beginning you hire a bunch of good people who are great at starting the company. But once the company turns a corner in size or scope, not everyone who was in at the beginning can turn that corner.

"You may have someone who, early on, when you're lean and dynamic, is a jack-of-all-trades, and that's what you need," he said. "But as each of those areas of responsibility grows, eventually you need to have one person focus on each area. And soon you strip away every job from that initial person—and there's not much left for him to do."

The same is true with management types. Someone who is an expert at handling a staff of ten or twenty may not be able to bear the load of a fifty- or one-hundred-person company. And at that point, Tim says, as hard as it may be, the entrepreneur has to make the realization that the fit may no longer be there.

"You're human and you think this person has been loyal and the company has grown successful with him, but in reality what you owe the shareholders and people there is to get rid of those people who got you started," he said. "It's harsh; it's the toughest thing you have to realize. But if you want to continue to grow and be dynamic, you can't be tied down to the limits initial employees place on you."

This doesn't apply just to employees but to partners as well. In his telecom company, Tim had a lot of partners, the initial criterion for which was whether they were college pals. As the company grew fast into a multi-million-dollar affair, it became clear to him that the responsibilities had outgrown the partners. But, because of the "club" atmosphere of the initial setup, it became hard to gently show partners who were liabilities to the door. After all, how awkward is it to fire an old friend, especially when other friends will remain in the business, and when those same friends comprise the social circle the entrepreneur travels in as well?

In fact—and he had the unusual asset of his own start-up capital with freightquote.com—for his present company, Tim made the conscious decision not to have partners, just investors. Employees and management, after all, can be managed and grown, or else let go. Partners are there for good, usually.

As for clearing the decks as the company grows, that presents its own challenges. "One problem is you usually notice that the company has outgrown a person six to nine months before you actually take the person out, because in part you're thinking you can make it work and you want to be a good, loyal employer," he said. "But eventually you start realizing that things will get worse if you don't execute on that revelation." He's had to deal with this on several occasions, and it cost him in terms of frustration and company growth.

The first problem Tim had was with his second employee at freightquote.com. "I knew he was a good jack-of-all-trades, and that's what I needed," Tim said. "But as we grew over the first nine months, we started having to take things he was doing and give them full-time to new employees, and eventually we got to the point where he had only one job left instead of the palette he started with, and the job wasn't one he liked. It got really uncomfortable because he started trying to get back involved with responsibilities other people had taken over."

Similarly, Tim held on to his first IT person far too long. The person was actually the third employee of freightquote.com when it started up. He was a genius at what he did—an IT entrepreneur, so to speak. But he was not an IT manager.

As the company grew, the IT genius started having an entire group of IT workers to oversee, and he had no real management ability, just seniority and legacy. And that can make things even more uncomfortable when a professional management type is brought in from the outside. It's hard to make a person go from quasi-manager to just another employee, and in a sense, the seniority aspect inadvertently undermined the new manager. He was another person who Tim got rid of at least nine months after his expiration date.

The third worst-case scenario that Tim faced came with his human resources person. A carryover from his initial telecom company, she was excellent at the early stage when the company's roster of employees could fit on a 3" x 5" index card and little sophistication was needed in the benefits administration. But as the company grew beyond one hundred employees, increasingly the HR director was in over her head.

"I was faced with the challenge of trying to keep this person out of loyalty and knowing we needed better management above her," Tim said. "But you can't just say, 'Hey, you've done a great job being the boss, but here's your new boss.' Instead of getting rid of this person in a positive way when I could have, I waited until things were on fire."

In hindsight, he would rather have gotten rid of her sooner than having had to force her out at the end of a pitchfork.

Today, Tim takes a more pragmatic and direct approach to employment and partnerships, and his company is dynamic precisely because he won't hesitate to bring an infusion of new blood in every six or twelve months.

LOST:

The opportunity cost of hanging on to employees that slowed the company down. Although not measured in exact dollars, having the wrong people probably cost Tim hundreds of thousands of dollars.

WHAT HAPPENED:

IT'S NOT PERSONAL, IT'S BUSINESS.

Friends are friends and business is business, and rarely should the two intersect. If you're interested in growing a company, not just maintaining the status quo, you can't be in a situation where emotional ties override what is good for the company. By bending over too far for the benefit of an employee or partner who can't grow with the company, you are hurting the rest of your employees and partners.

YOU CAN'T MAKE A PERSON GROW BEYOND HIS OR HER REACH.

More in a start-up than in any other kind of business, the people you hire or partner with have to know up front that their places are not set in stone, and if they can't grow into the job as it grows, there won't be a place for them. That goes for all levels—a trade-out of management can make a company all the more dynamic and prevent it from resting on its laurels. The opportunity cost of not changing leadership is great.

"One thing I think you should do is make a person re-interview for the job every year," Tim said. "Make your employee realize that comfort is not a goal. Growth is."

Steady and stable management is good if all you want is steady and stable performance, instead of dynamic growth.

"In hindsight you wish there were a temp agency for start-up executives," Tim said. "There are distinct stages and differences between a growth company and a stable, mature company."

Being honest up front about the lack of job security, and generous with severance, can ease the natural human guilt one feels. Face it—it's hard to sever ties with some-one. But what comes first is the company and those who are making it work.

QUESTION:

Are you hiring with a long-term vision? If you project fast sales growth, can your new hire handle that position in three to five years?

DIANNE PATTERSON

From an outsider's perspective, there's a lot about Dianne Patterson's life that seems counterintuitive. She was educated as an art teacher yet went on to found a multimillion-dollar insurance claims processing company. Her Meyers-Briggs personality test shows the exact opposite results for the standard CEO type. She built her business around managing people, yet it was the management of two senior people that became her biggest challenge.

But then, if being a successful entrepreneur were about taking the expected path, we'd have more chiefs than Indians.

Dianne attended the University of North Texas, where she studied art education and met and married the man who became the love of her life, Don. To help pay her way through school, she processed health insurance claims—an easy way to make money working from home. After graduation, she got a job with the Dallas school district.

One week later, she turned in her resignation.

"I just wasn't mean enough for what they wanted me to do," Dianne said.

Jobless, Dianne went with what she knew. She got a job with Equitable Insurance. She was more than a whiz at it—she perfected the "art" of claims adjudication so well that she was asked to be a third-party administrator for three agents who wanted to get into the claims administration business.

It was a very entrepreneurial environment and it prepared her for what was to come. But it was uncomfortable in one measure because of the seasonal nature of the work and the resultant hiring and firing slews the company had to go through to get the claims processed. The entrepreneurial mindset was starting to take hold. Rather than leaving it be, Dianne started looking for ways to resolve the problem.

"We were in a state of flux all the time—always hiring and firing people. So I came up with the concept of keeping a core staff of highly expert examiners that I would supplement with a core of temporary workers, all moonlighters," she said. "I came up with a discrete model of how to equalize the staffing levels even though workload varied greatly throughout the year."

It proved to be a success. Other insurance companies started wanting to borrow her team of temporaries. Her skill at management was becoming self-evident. Had things continued on an even keel, she might have ended up a successful middle or even senior manager for some large insurance company.

Instead, life threw her a curve ball. In 1980, the company took a nosedive, and the agents she was working for asked her to start laying off her core workers. It wasn't that she was afraid to cut people loose when necessary, but she had built a solid crew of highly skilled claims processors, and what they viewed as "expense cutting," she viewed as destroying a valuable asset.

Dianne took a leave of absence to consider an idea she'd had buzzing inside her head for some time. Her idea was to maintain her core and contingent workers, and form them into her own company to service market-wide needs.

"The original concept was to become the Kelly Services of health claims. During my leave, I called on two or three companies and hit them with the idea of using my contingent workforce during their unmanageable times. I called three companies and got three contracts," Dianne said. "So I went back to my job and resigned. The next day I incorporated what was then called Dallas Claims Services, later renamed Claim Services Resource Group."

Though she started small, on a citywide scale, she quickly realized that what she was building was highly exportable. The company grew from regional to statewide to national prominence. It was founded first as a highly specialized staffing company, but later added outsourced claims processing as its main service offering, thereby increasing profitability significantly. She grew the company from annual revenues in 1980 of $57,000 to approximately $65 million at the time of sale of the company in 2001 to Perot Systems of Dallas.

"With each new change in the industry there was an ever-increasing demand for the skills that we represented. What I was able to do was create and innovate a service in what turned out to be a narrow but very deep niche. It really carried us forward and we were able to reinvent ourselves every few years to become what the industry needed," Dianne said.

As far as Dianne is concerned, there are three things a leader is managing when he or she is in a service business—ideas, money, and people/talent.

"And I found by far the most difficult thing to manage is the people side of it," she said. "And the most important thing I learned is that when it comes to people and talent, what got you here won't keep you here or take you to the next level."

Dianne subscribed to the lesson many entrepreneurs swear by—fire early and often.

"I could tell early on if someone was not a match for my culture, and I'd cut a person loose at the first sign of a problem," she said. "But the trap I fell into was keeping someone long past when he or she was productive."

In a nutshell, by the early 1990s, the company had grown in both diversity of service and volume of work, beyond the capabilities of some of those employees who helped form the core senior management back in the early 1980s.

"It's quite a transition to go from managing a contingent work-force that works out of clients' offices to running a self-contained service center operation with a workforce under your aegis twenty-four hours a day," she said. "But you're never going to have a senior employee come to you and say—'I can't handle any more. I need help. I need someone to help oversee me.'"

"As we reached the $30 million revenue mark, it became too much for two women, Janet* and Sally*, to handle. They were good up to about the workload and scope when we were a $20 million company, and after that they became good at obfuscating their shortcomings," Dianne said. "We had invested a lot of money in setting up these service centers that ran twenty-four hours a day, processing claims for dozens of clients, and they could keep the work running in the service centers, but they weren't able to go out and get the new work.

"They kept on assuring us the work was coming in but it wasn't," Dianne recounted. "All of a sudden we were in a crisis. We had 400–500 workers in these centers, and long-term leases, and overhead that we couldn't afford unless they were at full capacity. But we were running at half-full, or a quarter. All of a sudden we went from being very profitable to being barely profitable. By the grace of God we were able to pull out of that downward spiral."

Dianne said her gut was telling her something was very wrong, but she couldn't narrow down what the problem was. Her first solution was to "professionalize" her sales force. Janet and Sally, who'd been with the company since its early days, had been in charge of sales and operations for the center in question, but they didn't have the kind of professional background a company pulling in $30 million a year necessitated. Dianne found two highly skilled, high-volume sales professionals at a Texas company—EDS, Inc.

"They got us back on course fairly quickly, but it left us with a very different kind of senior management group that wasn't at all cohesive," Dianne said. "They were used to working for a very professionalized management organization, and our core group was somewhat insular."

So while Dianne set about trying to forge the senior management back into one team again, Sally and Janet—mostly through incompetence, but possibly also with malice—set about sabotaging the two new saleswomen.

"Sally and Janet became very territorial. They went from actively trying to make things work to actively sabotaging the new sales team," Dianne said. "The two new women from EDS would sell a big contract—but Janet in the field was overstaffing existing clients so that we didn't have the qualified personnel available to staff the new contract."

For a couple of years the company sold 60 percent more contracts than it could staff. That shortfall was a huge hit to the bottom line.

"I had to fire Janet and close down that operation and bring it under our aegis in Dallas. We automated and professionalized the system so we could see and manage where each contract was coming through the sales funnel. That way we could more closely align staffing to contracts to make sure we had the skills inventory to service them once the contracts came through the sales funnel. By aligning staffing and sales, it solved that problem," Dianne said.

Then came the servicing crisis. Sales were running like crazy and Dianne and her COO had finally put staffing and sales in balance. And this time it was Sally who was overservicing clients, to the detriment of other contracts.

"So we had to automate and create servicing standards for clients. Once we took over management we had to guarantee servicing levels, quality, and accuracy in ways we didn't have to when we were providing hourly services," Dianne explained. "When our processors were working under the client, out of the client's offices, the flow of work and management was in the client's hands. I guaranteed them a qualified person—the client managed the people. But in the service center we had to guarantee quality and quantity of work."

Poor servicing eroded profits, and for a while a $30 million company, growing into a $60 million company, saw a correction that put it back to $15 million in revenues.

"Once the professionalized servicing system was in place, I could track individual employee productivity from minute to minute and see where we were failing. Sally couldn't handle the proactive needs of the automated control and management of servicing. She was unable to function in new ways. She could not adapt. After the servicing was professionalized, Sally took a position assisting the COO," Dianne said. "I was able to get her across the finish line, but it took her swallowing her ego and stepping down from what she had seen as her own little empire within the company."

A few years later, at its height of $65 million in sales, Perot Systems acquired Claim Services Resource Group. Dianne and Don now reside part-time in Carmel, California, and part-time in Dallas. Life is good.

LOST:

$10–$15 million over a three- or four-year period.

WHAT HAPPENED:

GET A PERIODIC FULL CHECK-UP—DON'T JUST GO TO THE DOCTOR WHEN YOU'RE SICK.

Dianne's company went through the growing pains any company will, skyrocketing as it did from less than

$100,000 in sales in year one to $30 million just a decade and a half later. The company was able to reinvent its services regularly as the insurance industry changed, but Dianne never bothered taking a holistic look at how the company itself was run.

And when you grow from six figures to eight, the way you do business is going to have to change.

"I had hired some outside consultants from time to time, but I always only pointed them at whatever problem we had at the time. I never had someone take an overall, strategic view of what was working in the company and what wasn't," Dianne says. "Luckily my problems happened sequentially, not all at once."

YOU CAN'T ALWAYS DANCE WITH THE ONE THAT BRUNG YOU.

Sometimes a job can outgrow the person doing it. You have to be able to do one of three things for that employee:

1) Provide the training the person needs to handle the growing scope, scale, or diversity of his or her position.

2) Convince a person to stay with the company as it turns the corner to the next phase of its growth, which means he or she may have to take a subordinate position to someone else.

3) Let that person go.

"It's a hard thing to do but you have to sit down and have a heart-to-heart talk about the employee's putting his or her ego aside and stepping down from one position to another one, but it is worth it," Dianne says. "In twenty-two years I never had anyone come to me and say, 'I can't do this job any more. I need help.'"

"It's in fact the hardest thing to do in my experience. But if I had to needlepoint a pillow with the biggest lesson I learned, it's that those who got you here won't keep you here or get you to the next level—you have to constantly hire up. That is not a peaceful, graceful thing, but it's the truth," she says.

QUESTION:

Has your company outgrown its processes and people? Do your employees have too much on their hands?

Have you taken stock of your company as a whole to determine what you are doing right and what you are doing wrong?

Are you doing right by your employees in letting them coast instead of either challenging them to grow beyond their limits?

Names changed for confidentiality.

JEFF TAYLOR

NAME: JEFF TAYLOR

CURRENT COMPANY: MONSTER.COM

INDUSTRY: ONLINE JOB RECRUITING

ANNUAL REVENUES: $550 MILLION

A lot of people like to say, "I'm a people person." Few can back it up like Jeff Taylor. This is a man who, although his business is touched by almost eight million people a day and he can't go anywhere without meeting someone who is a satisfied customer, doesn't feel like he's in touch with his customer base to the degree he'd like to be. It's part of the reason why despite being a millionaire many times over, he enjoys dee-jaying at parties and clubs—so he can interact directly with people and physically observe his influence on them.

And when Jeff says his greatest satisfaction in business is helping develop the careers of those he works with, he's not just blowing smoke. Jeff's company is synonymous with career development—Monster.com is the largest job and recruitment site on the Web, and it's his baby. So when a man like Jeff admits he's made a few mistakes in personnel issues, the wise entrepreneur listens intently.

Back in the early 1990s, long before dot-com had entered the common lexicon, Jeff owned a thriving, forty-person advertising agency named Adion. It was a successful venture, but like most entrepreneurs, Jeff kept his eye on the horizon. He started to develop an idea combining his own previous experience in the corporate recruiting world with this newfangled Internet thing. He did this within the aegis of Adion, but rather than taking his most senior people and most talented employees to work on Monster.com, he put his younger up-and-comers on the job. Which, in and of itself, was not a misstep. Heck, Jeff himself admits that the idea for Monster.com wasn't that popular initially within Adion.

"I knew I had to keep the ad agency successful while developing this new idea," Jeff said.

While Monster.com was under development, Adion continued to thrive, garnering the attention of advertising/communications giant TMP Worldwide. In 1995, Jeff and TMP Worldwide reached a deal, and both Adion and Monster.com were sold to TMP Worldwide. The problem is, for whatever he gained, Jeff had lost sight of his most valued resources, his employees.

While Jeff joined TMP Worldwide to head up Monster.com, his Adion employees were spread out and lost in the multi-billion-dollar mega-company, TMP Worldwide. Within six months, he started getting word that many of his senior Adion people were leaving TMP Worldwide. While Jeff and the crew from the original Monster.com had stayed together, the Adion employees, who were his most senior and important, felt left out. Not only was TMP Worldwide losing strong talent, but Jeff was also realizing he'd lost some important relationships.

"What started out as an effort to protect our reputation by keeping the original talent ended up pushing them into the arms of our competition."

In fact, he directly called two of his former Adion staff when he heard they were leaving TMP Worldwide, and he tried to offer them positions within the Monster.com division. Both said that he should have called them six months before. One left; the other accepted his offer.

"I should have been more aware of transition, been more sensitive to where they were," Jeff said. "We couldn't have afforded them all at the time, but I could have made them aware that I did want to continue our relationship and would work to bring them aboard later."

Jeff figures that of his valued Adion employees, he's managed to bring about one-third back into the fold at Monster.com, but the others have gone on to other careers and companies. The regret in his voice when he mentions this couldn't be more sincere, as is the sensitivity he has to his original crew. That sensitivity has grown even though today Monster.com employs more than 2,400.

Jeff's other biggest mistake came during that time of elation in 1995 when he sold Adion and Monster.com to TMP Worldwide. In fact, the primary asset in the sale was Adion—the sale of Monster.com was almost an afterthought for TMP Worldwide. In 1995, Jeff looked around himself and made a decision common to many entrepreneurs.

"You really are getting more paranoid as you progress up the mountain. You keep thinking, 'Well, there's no way I could do much better than this,' and you worry about falling off," Jeff said.

"But the reality is you keep doing better. I sold both businesses in 1995 for about $4 million. How could I know that it would boom in the next five years?"

The cliché that says timing is everything is always true. Jeff even points out he's seen the same thing in reverse, such as is the case with Web news streamer PointCast.

"I know that with PointCast, Murdoch or one of the other big media firms was at one point offering $450 million, but the management wanted to hold out for more. I read recently that three years later they finally sold for about $8 million," Jeff said. "They learned the same lesson in reverse."

Monster.com itself sold for less than $1 million on its own. Today, on a good day, Monster.com has a cap rate of about $2.5 billion.

Lest any reader feel the need to take up collections to help Jeff out, he did all right. In the contract for selling his company, he included a small clause that said if he helped take the company public later, he would, in return, get a small percentage of the business—1 percent, to be exact. Given that Monster.com is a $2.5 billion company, Jeff is bemused and understated.

"I did pretty good," he said.

Today Jeff continues to run what is now called Monster Worldwide—opening new offices in exotic locales, developing new ideas, dee-jaying in clubs for fun, keeping his eye on the horizon, and staying in touch with what he considers his most important capital—the people around him.

LOST:

Immeasurable opportunity cost in human and financial capital.

WHAT HAPPENED:

BEING AFRAID TO TAKE CHANCES WITH HIS PEOPLE.

Jeff didn't put his most senior people on Monster.com in its development phase for two reasons—he wanted to maintain the performance of Adion in case Monster.com didn't work, and he didn't think they could handle the transition as well. What is entrepreneurship without risk? However, he had never bothered to explain to his Adion staff the reasons for leaving them behind.

"One of the results created out of all of this is that when I come up with new ideas and products, I now take the best or most senior people I have and put them on it," Jeff said. "It has made my own people more well-rounded, and more important, it has baked the idea of change into our management. People know they may not be in a certain job for very long, which is good. It keeps things dynamic."

LOSING TOUCH.

There's more than just warm fuzzies at stake when it comes to people relationships. You can lose talent if they are not happy. Jeff didn't realize he had neglected his employees as he had, and he has since come to appreciate helping develop the careers of his employees more than anything else he does.

"The numbers you make this month or quarter, that's not something you can carry into the future. But helping develop a person's career is. And there's more joy to that than the tangibles," Jeff said. "Making your numbers is important, it's the basis of your business. But after that you try to get to where you can give a lot back to your employees."

Needless to say, while he can't keep up with all 2,400 employees under him, Jeff goes out of his way to cultivate the careers of his most senior people and has created a corporate culture at Monster.com dedicated to the very business they are in—career growth.

EAT DINNER WHEN DINNER IS SERVED.

This is a complex one. Hindsight is always 20/20. The management from PointCast and Jeff could probably have some raucous arguments, and no one has a crystal ball to see when it is the right time to act when it comes to selling your business.

In fact, Jeff admits that Monster.com wouldn't be a $2.5 billion company today if he hadn't sold it when he did—he didn't have the experience or infrastructure to take Monster. com global. Could he have held out for a little more? Maybe. But the fact is, he wasn't content to settle on speculation. He acted to ensure his own success in the deal.

"People can be afraid of negotiating, and you may only get half of everything you ask for, but if you don't ask for it, you won't get anything," Jeff said. "Looking back, I could not have sold my business for more than my stock in TMP is worth now. But by adding that simple sentence into my contract about getting one percent of the company if I was able to help them go public, I didn't get left out of my own success story."

QUESTION:

Communicating the reasons for making major transitions is critical to keeping key employees loyal. Are you getting ready to implement important changes in your business? If so, are you keeping your valued people "in the loop" with respect to issues that affect their jobs so you can avoid a potential backlash? If you are getting ready to sell all or a portion of your business and you plan to stay on as an employee, do you have the appropriate incentive clauses in your agreement that assure you equitable compensation for growth and/or a potential IPO?

Section Three

When Good Partners Go Bad

CHRIS RYAN

NAME: CHRIS RYAN

COMPANY: ERAPMUS

INDUSTRY: TECHNOLOGY CONSULTING

ANNUAL REVENUES: $8.5 MILLION

Chris Ryan, now head of a consulting firm that teaches investors how not to make the mistakes he once did with his own technology company, smiled easily and spoke with a steady, slow Texas pace that belies his New York roots.

"There's tremendous wisdom in scar tissue," Chris said. "And my back has a lot of wood marks."

An entrepreneur from a family of entrepreneurs—he only has one sibling in all his nuclear family who doesn't own his own business—this University of Texas graduate and former tennis instructor got a lesson early on about the motivating power of fear and the satisfaction of self-reliance.

In a classic "throw him from the boat and he'll learn to swim" style, his father told him that after his first semester in Austin, he'd be on his own financially.

"I realized real quickly that if I was going to stay in college and enjoy a reasonable standard of life, I needed to get a job," Chris said.

Eschewing the usual student route of waiting tables or delivering pizzas, Chris turned his solid—but unfortunately not scholarship-worthy—skills at tennis into a business. He began teaching tennis for several Austin-area apartment complexes.

"I was seventeen or eighteen and pulling down $50 an hour. And back then the University of Texas cost about $16 per credit hour, so it was easy enough to afford to go to school and have a nice lifestyle," he said. "That gave me the entrepreneurial bug to the degree that it wasn't already ingrained in me—I saw that I could finance my life and enjoy what I was doing."

It was during his college days that he met the man who would be his future business partner—David*—a good friend who even early on was a great complement to his own personality and skills.

After college, both went their own ways. Chris worked in sales and management in the telecommunications field while David became a computer programmer. Years later, in the early 1990s, they got together, and casting security to the winds of opportunity, they established a network integration and services company focused around insulating computer systems.

"It was a slow start—I put about $150,000–$200,000 away to live off of as we got it going, and for a few years I lived off macaroni and cheese and paid my rent with American Express and Discover," he said sheepishly. "I think I'm still blacklisted with American Express.

"We came together, put funds into it, and realized we were a good balance. I was the front guy—sales, presentation, revenue generation—and he was more the ops guy. It was, it seemed, a good professional marriage," Chris recounted.

The company followed the fortunes and directions of the burgeoning and soon-to-explode technology industry. Huge companies like Raytheon, Parkland Hospital, Children's Hospital, WorldCom, and others would engage the partnership to do various high-tech integration, removal, and upgrade projects.

As the technology field blasted off, so did the company.

At its height, the company had about ninety-two employees and annual revenues in excess of $8.5 million.

"The great news about the mid-1990s was that the water was rising everywhere in technology. If you had a pulse, you could make money in technology. We all got a little crazy and fat," he said.

In 1997 Chris and David decided to diversify the company. They set up three divisions. And because they were so cash-heavy, they were able to grow it organically—without seeking outside capital. They created a recruiting division, a support group division, and an integration services arm.

Problems started not long after.

"The biggest problem was we had a false sense of the Midas touch," Chris said. "Being good at one thing doesn't mean you're good at other things. And a fair amount of ego and pride went into it."

And, as the line from the old Billy Joel song goes, "They started to fight when the money got tight."

"In a partnership there are marriage components—it's a real relationship and it's easy to get along when there is success. When success fades, cracks turn to gaps turn to chasms," Chris said.

When things are bad, those chasms can be counterproductive to the operation, recovery, or turnaround of an organization, making problems even worse.

Chris and David overextended the firm financially, overestimated their own success, and diluted the strength of the management team by having some of them running these other divisions.

"We got away from our core competencies—we were spending the majority of our time managing things we were not good at and lost focus on the stuff we did very, very well. In about fourteen months we overextended ourselves and had lost a lot of our relationships and momentum in growing our business," he said. "I think that professionally there was too much on the table to manage and, frankly, a tremendous amount of ego and pride preventing us from seeing what was happening."

The reality was that the original model of the company did well—but the whole technology market was flourishing. It wasn't that their boat was rising, it was that the bay waters were rising.

Finally they had to take drastic action. The recruiting division was very labor intensive, so it was easy to shut the spigot off there. The opportunity cost was in management's time trying to get it going on the right track. The support division's infrastructure was about a $1.2 million investment. It included a $600,000 telephone switch that as a concept was a great idea, but when the rubber met the road, the demand for its service wasn't there.

"The expectation was that what was started with ten people would grow to one hundred, but we topped out at fifteen," Chris said. "It was the *Field of Dreams* mentality—build it and they will come. We assumed if the market would make itself available, heaven would open and the money would start pouring in."

By 1999, Chris and David were at serious odds, but they had managed to get the company back to its roots. They had taken on a lot of debt. In a short period of time, they'd gone from cash-heavy and $8.5 million in annual revenues to debt exceeding $3 million.

But all was not lost. There were a lot of acquisitions going on in 1999. A lot of non-technology investors wanted in on technology because they wanted to have bragging rights to having found the next Microsoft. A Houston company, VeriCenter, backed by a non-technologist who had founded Allied Waste and BFI, started talking acquisition.

"The high valuations they were giving were in expectations of a roll-up. They wanted to grab up several smaller companies and take it public and make a mint. The valuation we got was truly generous for what we had in place. We sold before the technology bubble burst and were able to address all of our debt, take some company money off the table, and even gain some stock in VeriCenter," he said. "We dodged an oncoming train. From start to finish we owed a lot to timing. And VeriCenter managed to weather the tech crash and make of our model a good business."

The end of the firm also meant the end of Chris and David as partners and friends. Too many stresses, disappointments, and miscommunications put asunder a personal and business relationship that had started as college chums and had risen to great heights of success.

LOST:

Millions in capital. Opportunity costs spent chasing business well outside their core competency. A fifteen-year friendship.

WHAT HAPPENED:

FIRST-TIME ENTREPRENEUR'S DISEASE—DON'T BELIEVE YOUR OWN HYPE.

At the heart of all entrepreneurs is—and has to be—the belief that whatever they can conceive and believe, they can in turn achieve. It's what gets them out of bed at 4 AM and fuels their twelve- to eighteen-hour workdays. It's what comforts them when they go to bed alone and wake up with the cold feeling of uncertainty that those who take the safer route of corporate employment never know. It's how they turn a great idea into a thriving business.

But that confidence should never give way to hubris.

"A friend of mine said that first-time entrepreneurs have okay vision, reasonable execution, and poor boundary setting in terms of our own skills and strengths," Chris says. "That's why we thought we could do anything."

You have to have the self-awareness to know your own strengths and weaknesses, and never let the fuel of your confidence burn down your objective self-assessments.

IT WAS MORE A BLIND DATE THAN A WELL-PLANNED MARRIAGE

Assuming you spend about twelve hours a day working, you're likely going to spend two-and-a-half times more hours with your business partner than your spouse.

Chris didn't want to go into the details of the erosion of the partnership but he did talk about how it got started on the wrong foot.

"I would have done a better job of setting expectations and boundaries and having a clear understanding between my partner and me," Chris says. "Because we weren't meeting each other's expectations, and because of the stresses on us in trying to turn around the company after we'd gone down the wrong path, it undermined our trust."

It ties in to the first problem above.

"A lot of execution was being done, but not a lot of thought. We didn't challenge each other in ways we should have" Chris says. "We were at first both in this kind of manic state—cash in the bank, market going great—so we never put in the thought to figure out what we really expected of the diversification or of each other. When things went south, so did our relationship."

Anyone looking to start with a partner needs to make sure that the aggregate value of bringing in that partner is greater than his or her own individual value. That means one plus one needs to equal ten, to be worth it. If one plus one only equals two, then there are going to be more problems than benefits.

Friends and family as business partners—there are often too many overlapping boundaries and expectations. It can be done, but it takes work, and it takes laying it all out beforehand and being sure everyone understands expectations. Misinterpretation of this yields to those cracks that come when things get tight or there are performance issues, and it invariably exacerbates the challenges of the business.

Today, through Paradigm Enterprise Solutions, Chris helps advise on fixing or putting to bed underperforming technology companies for investors. He calls it "company triage," built around the four precepts he believes must be sound for a business to be successful: management, customers, cash flow, and technology/widgets/hardware/software.

In a sense, he makes his way by showing his clients his own scars and lessons learned.

Everyone is going to make a mistake—from the first-time entrepreneur to the cover stars of Forbes magazine. It's how you deal with the mistake that determines your mettle and your future.

QUESTION:

Do you and your partner have a very clear understanding of your own expectations and goals? Is your relationship ready for rough waters?

And when you are considering growing outside your core competency—is that realistic, earned confidence driving it, or do you believe you are King Midas?

Hard questions in both cases—one speaks to the issue of your closest compatriot, the other speaks to your very soul. But if you're going to be successful—you must find those answers.

Name changed for confidentiality purposes

DAVID MATTHEWS

NAME: DAVID MATTHEWS

COMPANY: AV4U*

INDUSTRY: CORPORATE AUDIOVISUAL SERVICES

ANNUAL REVENUES: $22 MILLION

Someday, an innovative social scientist or psychologist will examine the apparent correlation between a person's exposure at a young age to the smell of fresh-cut grass and his or her likelihood of becoming an entrepreneur. Maybe it's something else, but suffice it to say, it seems to be a commonality among business leaders.

David Matthews, like so many grown-up entrepreneurs, got his first taste of building a business by pushing a five-horsepower lawnmower—mowing yards for money. While an undergraduate student at Ohio State University, he started an annual trade show that continued well after his graduation. And on the very same day he started his MBA program at Southern Methodist University in Dallas, David started an audiovisual company, AV4U.

But of course, it was not a smooth ride from the baseline to the top. He took more than his share of spills.

In 1991, entering the MBA program at SMU as a full-time student, David joined with one and then a second partner—two brothers— to form a company that provided audiovisual services for corporate meetings and events, as well as installing video conferencing and audio equipment for business clients. It was an equal one-third/one-third/one-third partnership, with each handling his own area of expertise. David oversaw business and financial management and also managed the company's sales and installation unit. The first brother, Tim*, managed the startup company's events staging operations, while Tom* oversaw marketing and studio production.

The company came out of the gate like a gold-medal sprinter, signing up one Fortune 1000 company after another.

It was growth they'd only dreamed possible. In 1991, they posted $150,000 in revenue. By the end of 1996, they were grossing $15 million, with 20 percent cash flow margins. Almost all the growth was funded internally, with just a few acquisitions.

As the business grew, the company units grew more distinct: product sales and installation, studio animation and visual production group, and events staging. Product sales generated the bulk of revenues, but at lower profit. Events staging was the company's cash cow. The visual production group was the company's loss leader—but it did serve the purpose of getting clients in the door.

The partners worked well together. Each had strengths to leverage against the next partner's weakness, and they generally had a strong common vision. A few things David saw should have been red flags— issues pertaining to personal integrity—but he let them slide.

"A partnership is difficult thing because you may have different goals," David said. "We'd been lucky to this point because we worked well together. I had seen some bad qualities in Tim and Tom, but the good qualities they had outweighed any other perception."

By 1996, the company had attracted the attention of outside investors, and one of their clients—a publicly-held software company—wanted to commit several million to the growth of AV4U. However, it was predicated on two conditions. The first was the usual requirement to meet certain performance marks. The second was that the software company investors wanted to bring in senior management from its ranks to ride herd on the three young entrepreneurs who, to this point, had built AV4U into a $15 million company.

Specifically, they wanted to bring in a new chairman, CEO, and CFO to oversee business, and leave each of the three entrepreneurs in charge of the three business units, which by this time had a combined total of more than 150 employees. Soon, trouble was brewing. For starters, the new chairman, CEO, and CFO quickly found themselves on a collision course with the three founders, particularly Tim and Tom.

"So we all went into this new relationship to grow the company seemingly on the same page," he said. "But we weren't."

One of the first things that happened was the new managers took a hard look at the studio unit—they thought it either needed a seasoned person to turn it around and make it profitable, or it needed to be shut down.

An effective studio executive from Boston was brought in and he worked magic, turning it into a profitable venture in no time. But Tom wasn't happy. He believed he was being muscled out and he didn't like having his baby taken away. He and Tim began to work actively to undermine the new studio unit manager. David saw this happening, and things deteriorated.

"Things eventually got so bad I went to have a conversation and create written documents with the new CEO, CFO, and chairman about how the brothers weren't being good team players," David said. "Although eventually we solved it and put water under the bridge, the relationship was deteriorating."

Six months later, working together, Tim and Tom forced the studio manager out, and at the same time they found a document David had written regarding his concerns about the two brothers. They decided he was trying to steal the company from them, so they decided to steal the company from David.

In short, it got ugly. Real ugly.

The dissention reached such a point that the chairman decided it best to divide up the company and spin off the sales, installation, and outsourcing unit—which David would own a majority share of—to be headed up by chairman himself. The two brothers would retain majority ownership of the studio and events units, which retained their name and offices.

The agreement reached was for a payout to the investors, to be paid out over several years as a percentage of AV4U's gross revenue. But Tom and Tim soon defaulted. They sputtered along for the first two years, paid out about 25 percent of the total payout, and defaulted on the rest as they disappeared into the night.

"They had too much debt to manage in addition to the payout, and it became more trouble than it was worth to go after them," David said.

LOST:

Several million in payouts to the shareholders, and all the potential a $22 million company would have had.

WHAT HAPPENED:

PARTNERSHIPS ARE HARDER THAN MARRIAGE AND CAN BE EVEN COSTLIER.

Partnerships are extremely difficult. Successful ones are so few and far between that they should be treasured and every step that can be taken to preserve them should be. You have to be careful of what may upset a balance—just like in a marriage. It's like having a mother-in-law move in—it's going to be a strain.

"We were successful in our first years and had a decent amount of mutual trust, but having outside parties come in and invest changed the dynamics of the whole mix and caused us to not be in alignment," David says. "If I had it to do again, I may not have taken the capital and just continued with AV4U as it was, but that's hindsight."

But also, the marriage of David, Tim, and Tom was never perfect to begin with.

"I had seen some bad qualities as related to honesty, but I let it pass because otherwise they did great and we worked well together," David says. "But at the end of the day, the bad qualities a person has will win out and can spoil what you build."

After all, a house built on a foundation that isn't solid isn't going to last forever. And this is an easy trap for an entrepreneur to fall into. Sometimes when a person is doing eighteen things at once—a typical day for an entrepreneur—it means they only have time to look for the good.

An entrepreneur has to be cautious in choosing and retaining partners. People are cautious about marriage and yet still half of all marriages end in ugly divorce and many more end up having infidelity issues. An entrepreneur trusts a partner with part of his future and with access to all of his resources.

"Also, with a partner—learn to partner on small things at first. Get transactional experience. Test the waters," David says.

It didn't take long for this serial entrepreneur to snap back, though. Today David is a director of a private equity fund investing in privately held growth companies, mainly in Texas and the Southwest.

QUESTION:

Are you in a partnership that needs more capital? Have you analyzed how this new money—and any stipulations that might accompany it—might affect the dynamics of the relationship with your partners?

Company name and brothers' names changed for confidentiality purposes.

Dr. Judith Briles

NAME: DR. JUDITH BRILES

COMPANY: THE BRILES GROUP, INC.

INDUSTRY: HOTEL DEVELOPER

ANNUAL REVENUES: NOT AVAILABLE

In some form or another, a common thread among otherwise successful entrepreneurs is that they miss doing their due diligence. Judith Briles's story of betrayal and embezzlement resulting from her own inattention is similar in many ways to those of other entrepreneurs who didn't keep their eye on the ball. But the lesson she learned and the way she turned defeat into victory is rather different. It may not be the right solution for everyone facing a difficult obstacle, but it's one every entrepreneur should consider.

It was the early 1980s. The economy was coming out of the Carter recession. Money was flowing and the business environment was coming alive again after the malaise of the late 1970s. In California, after several years as a successful stockbroker, Judith had become a savvy financial planner and investment fundraiser for a number of real estate rehabilitation and renovation projects. She and a partner Kerri*, who had worked together on several profitable projects before, identified a hotel in Berkeley, California that presented an opportunity for renovation. With a bank to back them on the construction project, they got to work renovating the property with hopes of reselling it for a hefty profit.

What followed would, if it were in a movie, seem more like a caricature of the 1980s than a real-life event. But it all happened. Judith's partner Kerri got caught up in the cocaine craze of the early 1980s, when the drug became not just a disco recreation but a daily, almost socially acceptable booster for the business set. To fund her habit, Kerri started nicking money from the bank by doctoring or forging invoices. The bank, displaying all the attention to detail of the later S&Ls that collapsed, approved the dispersals without a glance.

To give one an idea, the bank without hesitation approved and paid an invoice for $45,000 for "landscaping." This for a hotel situated between a bank and a grocery store with nothing but parking lot around it.

"They weren't paying any attention," Judith said. "But neither was I."

Within six months, Kerri had embezzled more than $450,000 from a loan that Judith and Judith alone had personally guaranteed. To this day Judith doesn't know whether that money was stashed away or if Kerri just snorted it all up her nose.

"And yet, I got nailed for it. Kerri declared bankruptcy and just walked away, and at the time the state's attorney said it would be too difficult to pursue charges against her," Judith said.

What followed were several years of litigation and wrangling in which Judith lost more than $1 million of her own money. She and her husband had to sell the house and even their clothes to make sure that their children were taken care of.

"We had to have a family pow-wow and tell the kids they could lose everything. We told them they would be cared for and fed but not necessarily in the style they were accustomed to," she said.

Early in the process, Judith sued the bank for their lack of diligence, and they ended up offering to settle before the papers had even been served. Instead of taking the money and putting it into her own account, Judith put it back into the investment fund. One of the creditors hired a shark attorney who ended up draining it all before a final settlement could be made. This went on for years, with Judith in court up to three times a week. Despite the bank's settlement, Judith ended up losing her personal assets. But in the end, she paid off every creditor at one hundred cents on the dollar.

Through the whole thing, Judith burned with one question— how could this have happened? She was an intelligent, successful woman. An MBA. A financial hawk. How in blue blazes could she have been taken so?

Astonishingly, despite all that was going on in her life at the time, Judith's burning question and the need to learn how to manage the whole renovation project with the hotel drove her back to school to work on her Ph.D. in business administration, with a special concentration on behavioral sciences. She was going to find out how and why she had been so easily taken to the cleaners.

Her study on the subject led to one of her first books: *Do Women Undermine Women?*

"The whole experience took me in a different direction," Judith said. "It reaffirmed for me that I didn't want to work with other people's money any more. It underscored that what I really wanted to do was educate people on how to handle their money and how to handle their business interactions."

Judith thought she had been pursuing her dream, but when reality came crashing down, it made her reevaluate her goals and desires. It brought to her the realization that she no longer wanted to work in the field she had been in. This was not a case of an entrepreneur backing down from a challenge, but rather one learning from a challenge to reorder her values and goals.

Thus was launched the career of Dr. Judith Briles—business consultant and award-winning author of more than twenty books on business relationships and business strategies. She also leveraged her experiences and knowledge into motivational speaking, delivering her programs with content and humor, and focusing on workplace solutions based on common sense strategies. The Briles Group, Inc., today is considered a leading workplace strategy consultancy with an impressive client list. Judith is a national director of The WISH List and is a past board member of the National Speakers Association, the Women's Bank of San Francisco, and the Colorado League of Nursing. Judith is an honorary member of the Association of Women Surgeons and The Women Officers Professional Association.

Judith wholly changed tracks to find her entrepreneurial success. This distinction is critical, because the last thing this book is intended to do is dissuade an entrepreneur from his or her dream or say it is okay to walk away from challenges. Quitting is rarely the ideal solution, but there's no point in playing a game you realize you no longer enjoy.

LOST:

Several years of happiness, mental well-being and more than $1 million.

WHAT HAPPENED:

IT'S BUSINESS, NOT PERSONAL, SO LEAVE TRUST OUTSIDE.

Judith was just too trusting. She considers trust both a great asset and a liability. And, as she proved through her own research, part of it was because she is a woman.

"Women are more inclined to give their trust. If it gets violated, they are willing to give someone another chance. Men don't do it that way. Kerri and I had previously done several projects together. So I trusted her."

In an odd way, she says, she learned there is wisdom in the old Mafia movie line, "It's not personal, it's business."

"I never confronted her on things. Aside from being business partners, I considered her a friend. And looking back, I realize that clouded my judgment on things that should have been red flags."

Clues were there that Kerri was having problems, but Judith ignored them. The hotel was being rebuilt and things were moving along.

"Looking back, all the signs were there. Some days she looked like hell. She claimed insomnia. But at the time I was naïve about drugs and their effect. If I could do it all over again, I would confront any unusual behavior and start probing more. You can't be too suspicious when it's your personal liability on the line."

NO ONE IS GOING TO LOOK OUT FOR YOU BUT YOU.

It's so easy to push aside the paperwork and red tape—that's part of the reason people become entrepreneurs. They have bigger visions, and they don't want to deal with the minutiae. If they'd enjoyed combing over reports all day long, they'd have become CPAs and auditors, not wealth creators.

And there's no doubt the bank messed things up royally. They didn't do their own due diligence on dispersing funds. But so what? Judith's name was on the loan—no one else's. At the end of the day, it was up to her to watch how that money was handled, since she was liable for it.

"Things seemed to be going well, but what we didn't see was there were hundreds of thousands of dollars in liens from contractors and vendors who weren't getting paid. I didn't see these ridiculous invoices like the one for $45,000 for landscaping. If I could do it again, I would insist on a copy of all checks written from the bank against the loan. I would have paid attention to where the money was going and where it wasn't."

QUESTION:

Have you invested money with friends, family members, people whom you truly trust? Does this mean slacking off on normal due diligence? NO! Remember, "It's not personal, it's business."

Name changed for confidentiality purposes.

SANJAY SINGHAL

NAME: SANJAY SINGHAL

COMPANY: SEVERAL

INDUSTRY: SEVERAL

ANNUAL REVENUES: NOT AVAILABLE

If he weren't a successful venture capitalist, world-class poker player, and technology innovator, he could be a poster child for business mistakes. He could teach business failure. In fact, he has—he's been a guest lecturer at Cornell University, and the subject matter was how he killed his first business.

In fact, his story is so unique that this chapter departs from the usual format. Sanjay just has too many lessons to teach.

Sanjay came up with his first business idea while he was working on his MBA at Cornell. (Humorously enough, getting schooled at Cornell was an experience that he believes may have slowed him down on his way to entrepreneurial success, but that is another story.) He was at a party when someone innocuously asked— "Why is it you can get pizza and groceries delivered to your home but not movies on video?"

Imagine the comic-strip lightbulb suddenly appearing over Sanjay's head. One week later he had drawn up a business plan, and during the second year of his MBA program, he made the concept the subject of every project. Despite some reservations by professors, shortly after his graduation at age twenty-five, Sanjay launched a video delivery company in Toronto.

"They can teach you at Cornell how to run a company at a CEO level, but they don't teach you how to be in the trenches, operating a company and doing the PR and marketing," he said.

And so the mistakes began.

Sanjay didn't go it alone—he had a business partner, and the two of them hired a mutual friend, Robert*, to run the flagship store and handle operations. It took a couple of months, but soon they realized that Robert was—incompetent, to be polite. "Robert would say he was off to negotiate a contract and then I'd hear the next day from a friend that he was out on the golf course," Sanjay said.

Despite having an equity position in the business—often a great motivator for people—Robert was just shiftless. Things didn't get done.

Sanjay, being young at the time and naïve about how to handle people, confronted Robert. Robert made the usual promises and "I will's." But over the course of six more weeks, nothing changed. Finally, things came to a head and Sanjay gave Robert his walking papers.

LESSON:

There are all kinds of reasons not to hire friends.

"The best possible reason to hire a friend is because he is good at what he does. The worst is because you want to help him out," Sanjay said.

References don't get checked, it's harder to redirect—in so many ways it is just not worth it. And of course it's hard to fire a friend, violating another maxim so many entrepreneurs live by—when there's trouble, fire early and often.

"The general rule I now apply is 'Don't do business with friends unless you respect them for business talent, and even then, be prepared to walk away from the friendship,'" he said.

And it gets worse. Robert's brother was acting as the company's attorney, so one day after Robert was let go, the attorney called to tell Sanjay he was withdrawing his services. Two days later, "friends"—the quotations are intentional—started calling and expressing dismay with Sanjay for firing Robert. They called him everything, including a bastard, and they let him know he wasn't welcome in their old social group.

"Some friends stuck by me, but by and large they put enormous psychological pressure on me that I had done wrong by a friend. It made life very difficult for me," Sanjay said.

But Robert was not the main reason the video delivery business failed. In the end, it was a lack of marketing experience.

"We relied on a direct mail campaign where we expected a 50 percent response rate. A lot of people had looked at the business plan, even people at the business school at Cornell University, but none had told me that the typical response to direct mail is between one half and 2 percent," Sanjay said.

Surprisingly, Sanjay actually bucked the odds and got a 10 percent return on his direct mail, but that wasn't enough to provide revenue, and they'd blown their marketing budget entirely.

So while they did come up with a way they believed they could save the business for an additional $20,000 investment, the partners decided to cut their losses—about $15,000 each.

LESSON:

Know what it is you don't know, and get that expertise.

"If I could have done it differently, I would have made sure I had all aspects of functional expertise in place to run the company—not just consultants and advisors, but people with equity in the company. I would have had people with me who knew what I didn't know about finance, operations, marketing, and sales," Sanjay said.

Sanjay wasted capital on the wrong kind of marketing, the wrong kind of people, the wrong kind of public relations, and the wrong kind of internal operations. It's little wonder he moved to California a year later.

In 1996, Sanjay took a job working for a company on the West Coast that made wireless data modems. A brilliant idea occurred to him—the Palm Pilot had just come out and he realized people might want to get their e-mails on their Palm Pilots. The answer? Simply marrying wireless modem and Palm Pilot technology.

Sanjay headed out to Silicon Valley, networked his behind off, and got a meeting with Jeff Hawkins, the founder of Palm Computing. Hawkins agreed to let Sanjay develop the hybrid technology, and Sanjay went about creating a prototype. He was

good with the technology but found he was not so good at getting financial backing. Time and again he was turned down, and
this was during the time when venture capitalists were almost
throwing money at technology and telecom ideas.

Out of the blue, during one of his many networking missions,
Sanjay met with the CEO of what was then a small, private
company called Novatel Wireless. The CEO was so impressed
he asked Sanjay to join Novatel. Soon enough, Novatel was
developing Sanjay's idea and Sanjay was heading up U.S. operations for the company—sales, marketing, and engineering. His
primary job was developing a marketing plan for the new product—Omnisky. The CEO was very pleased with Sanjay—in private he would even tell Sanjay that he expected one day Sanjay
would take over his duties.

"In developing the marketing plan, it got to a point where there was
a person I wanted to hire to work with me in San Diego," Sanjay
said. "But, unbeknownst to me, the COO of the company who was
feeling put off by the relationship I had with the CEO, decided to
veto my hiring decision. To have a decision like that vetoed really
bothered me. So I went to the CEO, who said he would take care
of it. When the COO found out I'd gone over his head, he immediately made an ultimatum—either I go or he would go. He'd gotten
wind I was chosen heir, and I'd pushed him into a public corner."

LESSON:

Don't ever push anyone into a corner unless you're planning on
killing him.

The CEO had a tough decision to make, and Sanjay knew what
it would have to be. As part of the severance, he received $50,000

for the rights to his technology patent. Eighteen months later Novatel Wireless went public—for $18 million.

"I believed everyone wanted to do the best job possible to advance the company rather than only focus on their own positions or careers," he said. "But most people seem to only focus on their own short-term status, rather than the overall good of the company, which in turn would benefit them anyway."

But it's all worked out.

After another failed company, bankruptcy, and two more moves, Sanjay ended up going into business with an old friend—for the right reasons. His friend and a third partner were starting up a company that makes voicemail software for telecom companies. Sanjay headed up sales and marketing, and for the first time in a company in which he had equity, he felt as if he weren't the only one propping up the company.

Unlike in his video delivery business, this time his two partners brought to the table the skill sets the others lacked—meaning, within their core partnership they had everything covered.

"The CEO handled engineering and operations, and the chief technologist is a brilliant software architect. Among the three of us we could solve any problem, where alone any one of us would fail miserably."

In the worst telecom economy imaginable, the company has doubled its size and sales every six months for the past four years. They have gone from first year revenue of barely $100,000 to $14 million. They project it will become a $100 million company in six years.

Sanjay sold his equity in the company and still acts as an officer in the company, but he has established his own venture capital firm, Aquanta Group, where he can explore new technologies and ideas from the side of the table he wasn't on when he was a mere developer. Each mistake and failure along the way to where he is now was taken to heart, and he fully exploited each lesson.

"It takes determination, a belief that you are right, and the kind of energy most people aren't willing to commit, but it can be done," Sanjay said. "Don't get too smart for yourself. You can accomplish your goals and become successful in spite of your intelligence."

QUESTION:

Thinking of hiring a friend in your company? Have you assessed whether his or her strengths offset your weaknesses? Are you prepared to walk away from that friendship if the working relationship turns sour?

Names changed for privacy purposes.

VALERIE FREEMAN

NAME: VALERIE FREEMAN

COMPANY: IMPRIMIS GROUP, INC.

INDUSTRY: TEMPORARY STAFFING

ANNUAL REVENUES: $30 MILLION

We've touched in this book on partnership problems, and this one has many of the same symptoms and causes as others, but with a little added lesson about the complications of friendships and family in business. We won't go back over covered ground, but we will try to underscore the cost of a bad partnership.

Valerie Freeman has had business partnerships like some Hollywood stars have had marriages—messy, costly, and ending with a lot of bad feelings.

Not that Valerie started out with the goal of becoming the highly successful businesswoman that she is today, but she always has been a take-charge kind of woman, and someone who likes to live on the forward edge of the curve. A former steel guitar player from Houston who used to race Corvettes for fun, Valerie moved to Dallas, after she completed her degree in the late 1970s, to join the faculty at El Centro College.

She was teaching business courses at the time when word processing was really taking hold in the business world. Well, she wasn't one to wait around—she was going to blaze a trail. Using her own money, she bought the necessary equipment, learned everything there was to know about the subject, and wrote the curriculum on word processing management.

The more she learned, however, the more interested she became in the technology and the less interested she became in teaching college. Throwing caution to the wind, she started her own company, training and placing people in the then-burgeoning field of word processing management—the first company in Dallas doing so. Today her concern has grown to more than seventy-five employees in six states, filling a number of data management niches.

But that's not to say the road to where she is now didn't have some major potholes. Her first partnership problem arose early on with this company.

"We started and we were running this company by the seat of our pants. It was all new," Valerie said. "What I didn't know is that, at the end of the day, my partner simply didn't know how to run a business."

Actually, that's a rather generous assessment. From the way she described it, it's hard to imagine that he knew what a "business" was.

"He had totally different ideas on how to spend money—he thought we should spend on lavish living and not save or invest it in the company," Valerie said. "He did not conduct himself professionally. He would roll in at 9 AM and leave at 3 PM to play tennis."

Valerie said the only thing that kept the business going for the year and a half that they were partners was her work. She was bringing in the contracts—he was, well, taking up space.

"He set me back a year and a half. And what was worse was how unpleasant it was for our relationship," she said. "He was a friend, and I lost total respect for him. We lost our friendship over it."

LOST:

A long-term friendship. Several hundred thousand dollars. A year and a half of business growth.

WHAT HAPPENED:

PLAYING A JACK AND A KING LIKE THEY'RE A PAIR.

He or she could be your best friend from childhood. Your old Army buddy. Your sorority sister. Your most trusted confidant. The person who pulled you from the bottom of a pool when you were kids.

But going into business, none of that really means a thing. If a ship is going to have two captains, they need to agree on the destination, the course, and how the bridge will be run. Otherwise, that ship is going to run aground.

It's been said time and again—you are being asked to trust each other and spend more time together than you will with your spouses. You better make sure you're both on the same page.

"I would say you really need to sit down and talk about expectations, job duties, how much business each is responsible for, what will it look like, hours, goals, objectives, etc., and leave no detail undefined," Valerie says.

Partnerships only work if both parties have the same goal in mind—for instance, getting the company to a certain level and then cashing out or going public or whatnot. Only then it can work.

Don't rush into partnerships or alliances without knowing where you are going. You can't fly by the seat of your pants. Write down your targets and your goals. Manage your relationship like a business.

HEY, IT'S JUST AN APPLE . . .

Unfortunately, "once bitten, twice shy" doesn't always apply to risk-taking entrepreneurs like Valerie. The second time she was bitten by a partner was during a side business venture in which she was a minority shareholder. Having learned her lesson about expectations, she made sure they were on the table and in writing.

The partner was a relative—a family man whom she believed she could trust. The business model was sound, and shortly into the venture, the company was posting revenues of more than $3 million, based in large measure on the contracts Valerie herself brought in. What could go wrong?

The details of the company aren't really important. The result is—somehow this "family man" who, as majority shareholder, had a personal interest in seeing the business thrive, actually ran the company into the ground. There were no overt warning signs—the point is that potential problems lurk even when you think you've done your due diligence.

"It was amazing. For the first couple of years everything seemed to be great," Valerie said. "What I didn't see was that this person had a serious leadership and ethics deficit. I wonder if he didn't have some sort of self-destructive psychological problem.

"There was no reason at first to think there was any creepy stuff lurking in the corner. But then employees started to leave. I began to see there was no direction or leadership from him. Then I realized there were bill collectors calling to collect on accounts I didn't even know about," she said. "Unbeknownst to me, credit cards were being maxed out and debts were incurred without my knowledge. Assets of the company were being used for another company that I did not even know existed."

The more she uncovered, the more she was flabbergasted.

"I couldn't believe he was such a goofball as to ruin a company that had so much potential," she said, shaking her head in disgust and bewilderment apparent even today. "I couldn't do anything about it after it started. I couldn't make this person do anything. I resigned off the board and refused to fund any more of the business and watched it go down the tubes."

LOST:

Half a million invested in the company. A $3 million company down the drain.

WHAT HAPPENED:

YOU CAN NEVER LET DOWN YOUR GUARD.

It's going to sound ugly, but the truth is there was little Valerie could have done to avoid this. And it's going to sound cold, but you can never trust anyone else as much as you trust yourself.

There were no deficits of due diligence. Valerie did everything right, though in hindsight she sees a few clues that might have given her pause.

But the fact is, polished sociopaths, clever liars, and self-destructive con-men have been fooling the brightest of people since the day a certain reptile convinced a certain naked woman, "Hey—it's just an apple, c'mon, take a bite."

You take risks in business—that's why there are rewards—but you have to take calculated risks. There are always some little indications of character flaws in people you do business with, and you can't ever ignore them when you are calculating your risks.

There were a few things Valerie could have done, however, to protect her position and her investment.

"If I could do it again, I'd say that there has to be a contract in place that if you don't maintain this certain level of sales or profitability, then you're going to have to divest yourself," she says. "As it was, I had no power after I realized there was a problem."

And even if you are the silent partner, you have to do more than just read the financial statements—those can be fudged. Talk to employees. Talk to vendors and clients. Is your partner late to meetings? Does your partner seem invested in the business at all times?

It should be the first commandment of business—cover your assets.

QUESTION:

Do you trust your partner as much as you trust yourself? Do you know your partner as well as you do yourself?

You've done everything to make sure that you know your partner's expectations, character, habits, role, and responsibility. Has he or she shown that same diligence? If not—is he or she really as invested in your partnership as you are?

Section Four

The Corporate Culture:
If It Ain't Broke . . .

KIP TINDELL

NAME: KIP TINDELL

CURRENT COMPANY: THE CONTAINER STORE

INDUSTRY: CHAIN OF RETAIL STORES

ANNUAL REVENUES: $370 MILLION

In 1978, Kip Tindell, along with his co-founder Garrett Boone, decided to open a store devoted to helping people streamline and simplify their lives by offering an exceptional mix of storage and organization products. Despite what "experts" considered a counterintuitive philosophy of employee involvement and compensation (employees earn between 100–150 percent more than retail industry average), and the additional challenge of persuading commercially oriented manufacturers to supply them with retail products, it caught on. In many ways better than they could have hoped. Kip and his partner wanted to be more than just a storage retailer—they wanted their store to be a solutions provider. And the popularity showed in the numbers: The company has seen 20 percent revenue growth every year since its founding. Indeed, sometimes the greatest challenge has been in *limiting growth* so that the focus on customer service is not lost.

Today, The Container Store boasts locations coast to coast, with stores ranging in size from 22,000 to 29,000 square feet, showcasing more than 10,000 innovative products. In every store, there's always someone in sight wearing a blue apron ready to help solve everything from the tiniest of storage problems to the most intimidating organizational challenges. The company's unique corporate culture of unlimited customer service, consistency, employee empowerment, and matchless product knowledge is almost palpable.

Kip has faced a number of challenges in helming The Container Store, but none so demanding as creating and maintaining that corporate culture.

"No matter what you do that is outside the norm, you will have a lot of doubting Thomases who think you shouldn't do it," Kip said. "Especially when you're just 25 years old and have no real experience, it can be hard to stick to your vision and to your principles. But when you know something is right, you have to stay true to it."

This is not to say that one shouldn't abandon an idea that is failing. Sometimes an entrepreneur has to cut his losses—be it an issue of marketing, personnel, or large capital investments that go awry.

In fact, Kip learned in 1984 that sometimes you have to hold fast while simultaneously being willing to completely cut your losses. It sounds contradictory, but what Kip learned was that he had to hold fast to the original vision for The Container Store while letting go of millions invested in a plan to computerize his network of stores.

"We came close to losing the whole business in 1983. We almost had to shut down," Kip said. "We had put three or four million— and that was a huge amount of money back then—into bringing technology into our operation. We hired the best consultants and bought the best hardware and software.

"And it was a massive failure," he said.

The problem was that The Container Store, in every aspect, had a very unique approach to how things were done. Employees were not just sales personnel but space consultants. And they were compensated accordingly. However—and one must remember this was more than a decade before software customization was common—in the rush to bring technological efficiency to the operation, The Container Store began trying to adapt its own methodologies to the software.

"And the result was it nearly brought us to our knees," Kip said. "Finally, we fired all but one of the consultants—the one who we realized knew how to get things done—and spent two years having a computer system built that was adapted to our vision. For two years in the interim, we went back to doing things by hand. It wasn't easy, but we recovered from that fiasco. We built the customized system and we've continued to build on that foundation."

The new system was a cyber mirror of the company's original methodology.

"It just underscored something we learned from a lot of challenges, ranging from growing too fast to mistakes with personnel issues— you have to have the courage to be true to your philosophy."

LOST:

Almost $4 million capital investment in technology, training, and systems.

WHAT HAPPENED:

EMBRACING THE NEW AT THE EXPENSE OF THE TRUE.

There's a revolution in how business is done almost every week, be it born of technology, management philosophy, customer service philosophy, investment strategies, or something else. And woe to the entrepreneur who doesn't recognize advantages in new methodologies. But when a new way of doing business detracts from the very foundation of what has brought success in the first place, the foundation is eroded and nothing can stand.

Contain the urge for revolution and think in terms of evolution. The smart entrepreneur adapts new ideas, new systems, or new hierarchies to his or her business, not the other way around.

Part of the problem was that it was a new paradigm—this whole computerization of business in the 1980s. But changes will be just as dramatic tomorrow. Kip should have, but did not, ensure that his consultants understood that The Container Store philosophy needed to be incorporated into the change.

QUESTION:

Have you identified your corporate culture? That unique part of your business that contributes to your success? Once identified, will you ensure that any major change you make within your company enhances, or at least supports, that uniqueness?

JOE CROCE

Joe Croce is well aware of what got him to the big dance. He started poor, smart, and hungry, and the first people he hired were the same. He was an entrepreneur who wasn't afraid to roll up his sleeves and get his hands dirty. Or rather, a little marinara-stained, as it were. Joe is the founder of CiCi's Pizza, a simple concept he started of an all-you-can-eat pizza buffet that he has grown into a success with more than two hundred franchises nationwide.

"In the beginning, we built equity with each other, the goals, the sense of purpose," Joe recalls fondly. "It was a unique culture we crafted."

Joe had people who worked hard, and his managers were the kind of people who thought like entrepreneurs. Joe and his crew were racehorses who led by doing. They followed the culture and model Joe had laid down at the beginning, and with determination it went from its humble beginnings to a company knocking on the door of half a billion in sales.

An ordinary businessperson would be happy enough. But the entrepreneurial mindset isn't wired that way. It always asks, how can I do this even better?

Joe started looking at other businesses—the ones who'd cleared the $1 billion-and-better hurdle.

"The problem is, despite all we do as entrepreneurs to carve out our own way of doing things, so often we are so vulnerable to an impression of how it must work based on how other people succeed," Joe said. "So even after fifteen years with a great company, I'd be likely to read a story in the *Wall Street Journal* or see a video about some company that was bigger than us and say 'Hey, I need to bring that kind of model to my company. I need those kinds of people.'"

And the fact is, sometimes that attitude is right. Sometimes a company can outgrow its people, especially when it goes through growth that is not scalable, but rather growth that is a paradigm shift. Until now Joe had "doers"—leaders and operations people who knew what it took to run restaurants.

But Joe thought what he needed were thinkers—the big picture leaders who would somehow bring more efficiency, a grander way to do things. Somehow he knew that if he brought in thinkers, he could achieve his goal of doubling his annual sales. So he went out and bought himself a thinker. He was a person Joe thought would have the instant knowledge and experience needed to leverage CiCi's Pizza to the next level.

The new chief operating officer Joe brought in—as much because of his impressive résumé and his marvelous interview style as because of his experience—was considered different from the culture CiCi's was built on.

That's when the trouble began.

The new COO was a sharp contrast to the rough-and-tumble racehorses who ran the CiCi's Pizza franchises. Joe figured that for a good thing. But it wasn't long before things started feeling wrong. The stores began to take on a less frenetic, more structured atmosphere. The reliance on store managers as a key ingredient in the concept's success lessened in favor of a more top-down approach that soon had older managers leaving and new, more malleable managers hired in.

"The thinker turned the stores into a mundane kind of no-energy place," Joe said. "Before, the troops used to say that they'd run through a wall for their manager, because that manager had been there and pulled it all together and knew how to handle the kind of unexpected things that happen in the restaurant business.

"The attitude among the staff about these new managers was they were blockheads who didn't know what was going on," Joe said. "There was no respect. The morale dropped. The turnover climbed. And of course it compounds itself because the thinker goes out and hires thinkers, because we hire in our own image. So now I've got a store full of thinkers. I need action, not thinkers.

"Thinkers aren't good at being reactive. Reactive gets a bad rap when it shouldn't. Proactive is great, but I need reactive in the restaurant business. There's a place for being proactive. That's during the week. But on Sunday, game day, you need reactive," Joe said.

So much in life and business is made of mistakes. No one can dream up a model and have it work without some blip. Some business models are more prone to blips—the restaurant business is one of them. In Joe's case, he needed the people who could make those blips, then brush themselves off and get back in the game. Instead, he had thinkers.

Within six months, all those intangible warning signs and bad feelings started to show on the bottom line. Turns out Joe had replaced his racehorses with pack mules.

"The reason it took time to manifest itself is because the old people were still hanging on to the old way, but then gradually there's turnover and new people are doing it the new, wrong way, and more old people leave because they are frustrated with new people, and soon the whole thing starts to collapse," Joe said. "Before you know it, you're a company of new, stinking thinking."

Joe had to go back to step one. He had to recognize what had built his pizza empire in the first place, and that while new blood can be energizing, an entrepreneur shouldn't tinker unnecessarily with a successful culture.

Or, as they say in Texas, "Dance with the one that brung ya."

It took a little time, but CiCi's is back on track, serving up success hot and fresh.

LOST:

Incalculable. At least six months of declined sales and six months of time rebuilding back to that level. Competent managers who fit the culture of CiCi's.

WHAT HAPPENED:

DON'T HIRE THE RÉSUMÉ.

This is where entrepreneurs get slapped in the face. When they see someone who is a head of a department in a large national or multinational corporation, they assume that the person must, perforce, know everything about that department. After all, that's the way it is with entrepreneurs, right?

Wrong. In fact that's often the furthest thing from the truth.

"They have people to do their nails," Joe said. "They may not know much of anything. The regional and district manager are the ones getting things done—the department head is the one talking to the analyst in New York, playing up the stock. Yet he is the guy you'd see in the magazine and say, 'Oooh, I gotta have him.'"

YOU CAN'T REMAKE A MANAGER.

Allowing for the fact that some industries are by their nature more frenetic and fast-paced, requiring hands-on leadership, the only way to ever give a "thinker" what he or she needs to be successful in such a company is to spend night and day with him, teaching him the culture and teaching him how to do every little job. But if you're building a company, you haven't got time to give him night and day. It is almost impossible to take a twenty-year corporate mentality and turn it into an entrepreneurial mindset.

YOU CAN REMAKE A MANAGER—TO A DEGREE.

No, this is not a contradiction. Joe originally had doers, but he thought he needed thinkers. So he got rid of some doers to make room for the thinkers, and you can see how that turned out. The thing is, Joe could have turned some of his doers into thinkers, but thinkers who could still do.

"Looking back, for a fraction of what my mistake cost me, I could have taken some of those racehorses of mine and sent them to the right classes and seminars so that they could bring that thinker mentality into the equation, without the cost of having a thinker who couldn't do," Joe said.

QUESTION:

Are you drooling over the résumé of an Ivy League-educated, Wall Street-trained, Fortune 500 executive? Do you know whether he or she has the character to fit into your corporate culture?

Section Five

Entrepreneurship 101

SAM HORN

NAME: SAM HORN

COMPANY: ACTION SEMINARS/CONSULTING

INDUSTRY: INDEPENDENT SPEAKER AND CONSULTANT

ANNUAL REVENUES: NOT AVAILABLE

Although national award-winning speaker Sam Horn is seemingly immune from failure, the biggest setback she has faced is one that isn't so uncommon, particularly in today's mercurial business world.

Sam's story is like a few others in this book, only it shows that not all setbacks are misfortune or bad decisions. Sometimes they are trades of value for value, but encompassing their own challenges.

A former athlete and tennis coach who worked with tennis pro Rod Laver on Hilton Head Island ("where I learned to lob a forehand shot with one hand and drink a Foster's beer with the other"), Sam had in the late 1970s established herself locally in the Washington, DC area as a business marketing consultant. From her humble beginnings talking to a mere sixteen participants, Sam grew her consulting business to a budding regional reputation with clients including major businesses and associations.

Then came the setback. Well, a setback in a velvet glove. Or white lace glove, to be precise. Sam got married and moved with her husband to Hawaii. All of a sudden she was a "nobody" again in a new market. No one knew who she was, and no one cared to know.

Okay, so maybe getting married and moving from about as far east on the East Coast to about as far west as you can go and still be in the United States isn't common.

But how many people these days are being displaced from their locales, and not by choice? How many budding entrepreneurs on the cusp of starting their own businesses but still tied to a company are being transferred hither and yon? Or perhaps the person being transferred is the spouse of the entrepreneur who is just getting the business off the ground? Or maybe the necessity for a move comes from a familial obligation.

Whatever the case, it's not uncommon for entrepreneurs to find themselves having to uproot and start from scratch in what is, for all intents and purposes, "foreign territory."

"It's not easy to go from successful and well-known to where nobody knows or cares who you are," Sam said. "But you can do it if you have a plan."

Sam is a big believer in "social savvy." Social savvy, talent, intelligence, and quality are all important, but those alone are no guarantors of success.

"People do business with people they know, like, and respect," Sam said. "That's just a fact of life."

So upon arriving in Hawaii, Sam set to work immediately on a very deliberate and well-thought-out plan.

"When in a new environment, we have to determine the quickest way to establish ourselves, and thus we have to ask who the decision makers we need to influence are," she said. "Then we have to take responsibility to make sure they know who we are, so that they can evaluate if they like who we are and if they want to do business with us."

"Above all, don't wait, initiate," Sam said. "We have to take 100 percent responsibility for putting ourselves in front of who we need to. No whining, no complaining or making excuses. Do not be derailed by daunting circumstances."

Sam doesn't believe in cold calling or knocking on doors. She approaches challenges with the methodical planning and study of a successful wartime general. She gathers intelligence about the battleground, about whom she will be facing and about what they expect.

"In my business, and in many others, the best approach to find the decision makers is through community and business organizations. What I try to do is get in there and secure a position that is both high-profile and offers autonomy—no committees or volunteer work, per se, but one that puts you in front of the people you need to be before, and still be in control of what you are doing," Sam said.

For example, when Sam recently moved back to the Washington area from Hawaii, one of the first things she did was approach one of her target associations and offer an all-day, pro-bono retreat and seminar at her home. While her motives were in her own best interest—developing new clients—she also approached the challenge with integrity.

"There is nothing wrong with pursuing your own interests, so long as what you offer in return is done with integrity," she said. "What I got from this was exposure, client referrals, and a development of word-of-mouth about my services, but it was important to me that I exceeded the expectations of those who attended, and offered them the best I could. "

Don't wait by the phone—put yourself in front of those you need to reach. Do it with integrity.

But back to Sam's challenge in rebuilding her business when she moved to Hawaii. The very first week she was there, she went to the University of Hawaii and pitched her "ConZentrate" class to add to the continuing education curriculum. Sam didn't do this cold. She was as well prepared as a signature item at a five-star restaurant.

"I did my homework. I knew when the deadline was for offering a new class for the curriculum. I made sure the class I was offering wasn't duplicating something they already had, and I wrote the course description in the style of the others. I found out who the decision maker was, and I knew that what he would say after we talked was 'Send me something.' So I had a one-sheet and a bio ready and I faxed it to him twenty seconds after we got off the phone, which sealed the deal."

Sam said the key in making such a pitch—whatever the business venue, whatever the industry—is to make sure every factor is primed for "yes."

"For instance, I knew that he would want something additional in writing, and if I put it in the mail it wouldn't get to him for three days, and who knows how long it would sit on his desk. And by the time he got to it, he would have forgotten who I was.

I made sure I got him what he needed while he was still fresh from our positive telephone conversation.

Anticipate what a prospective client, partner, investor, or customer will need, and have it ready. Anticipate by doing your research well in advance, thus priming the prospect for "yes."

The initial class enrollment was about thirty people, most of whom asked Sam to speak at their businesses or organizations.

Sam also put herself in front of the decision makers she needed to reach by working as a columnist for an organization newsletter. It was something she could do on her own schedule, and which granted her access in multiple ways.

"You can do this for most any association, whatever your business, or you can even do it for a community newspaper. If you can't write, you can make the column one where you interview the movers and shakers in the industry you are trying to reach," Sam said. "This gives you a legitimate excuse to be calling and getting to know the CEOs or leaders you are trying to be in front of, and they will start to recognize you as someone they enjoy speaking with. This builds your social savvy."

There is more than one way to get the attention of the decision makers you need to reach. Be creative.

Within a year of moving to Hawaii, Sam was earning her living as a speaker again. Over the course of the next twenty years, she provided workshops, keynotes, and public seminars for more than a half-million people across the country, and she authored four formidable books: *What's Holding You Back?*; *ConZentrate: Get Focused and Pay Attention*; *Take the Bully By the Horns*; and

Tongue Fu!® How to Deflect, Disarm, and Defuse Any Verbal Conflict.

"Initiative is the key for an entrepreneur. Anything that happens to you in a day should be the result of your efforts. If you are lazy and passive, nothing will happen," Sam said. "That idea, that empty slate, must make your heart sing. For some people that would be frightening and intimidating. But as entrepreneurs we see it as wide-open possibility and move forward eagerly rather than being overwhelmed and immobilized."

QUESTION:

Are you facing the possibility of a major life change? Do you have a plan in place that will allow you to quickly rebound, recover, and minimize financial losses?

CYNTHIA MCKAY

While some of the entrepreneurs presented have admitted that in one area or another they failed to do their due diligence, Cynthia McKay is not a person who falls directly into that group.

Cynthia is no novice when it comes to doing her homework. McKay studied art at the University of London, England, and received her BA degree from the University of Central Florida and her law degree from the University of Denver. She is, to say the least, one smart cookie.

And speaking of cookies, that brings up her business. Cynthia founded Le Gourmet Gift Basket as a small home-based business in Denver in 1992. It's a lot more than just cookies, of course. These are custom-tailored gift baskets with gourmet products suited to each recipient.

Le Gourmet Gift Basket, Inc., has expanded under Cynthia's direction across several states with 410 operating distributorships. She has developed the practical economics of a home-based business so that profit is high, overhead is low, and as a self-employed individual, morale is great. While Cynthia strives for the success of her own company, her efforts to help others succeed in their ventures have won her honors, including the Women in Business Advocate of the Year Award from the Small Business Administration, for her accomplishments in the development of business opportunities for women.

Cynthia has also received the American Association of University Women Trailblazer's Award for her accomplishments in business.

As stated before, this is not the kind of mind that makes due diligence mistakes or fails to read the fine print, right? Wrong.

A few years back, as her business expanded, Cynthia moved out of her initial offices in downtown Denver and bought a former gas company utility building, which she planned to renovate into a corporate headquarters.

Significant work needed doing, so Cynthia went out and shopped around for a contractor. She checked rates and made sure to ask if the contractors were licensed, bonded, and insured. Time to get to work.

Two months into the renovation, there was an accident. One of the contractor's employees was painting outside when he fell, sustaining some serious injuries. He claimed he slipped on a loose roof tile. Cynthia, of course, felt bad for the man but she knew it was an issue for the contractor to handle—after all, that's what licensed, bonded, and insured is there for.

Except, as it turned out, when the medical bills started rolling in, the contractor was not licensed, or bonded, or insured. He did not have liability or worker's comp. Oh, sure, he had said he did—even said so in his Yellow Pages ads and marketing brochures. The reality that a person can get a print shop to put anything they want on a brochure sank in all too certainly.

"It was absolutely deplorable. I did do my homework," Cynthia said. "Or so I thought."

Looking back, she realized that the insurance policy papers she had been shown were actually expired. And it turns out that while the contractor had at one point been formally incorporated, the incorporation had expired.

Out of nowhere, Cynthia was facing a worker's comp lawsuit, even though she had never directly employed the contractor's injured employee, and a liability lawsuit.

Well, the lawyer in Cynthia wasn't that concerned. Clearly the contractor was responsible—after all, he had misrepresented himself entirely—and further, the injured employee could in no way be linked to her company. And, in what she thought was further exculpatory evidence, blood tests of the injured worker showed a positive result for cocaine use. So as far as she knew, she had common sense, the law, and evidence of drug abuse all on her side.

That's when things got really interesting, in the Chinese sense of the word.

Cynthia soon discovered, to her absolute horror, that in the state of Colorado, the law holds that if a contractor doesn't have insurance or worker's comp, then the contractor's client is liable for any problems.

And more, the judge threw out the evidence of cocaine use, since the worker claimed the test was done without his consent. It was downhill from there—despite what she believes was obvious conflicting testimony and evidence of collusion between the injured worker and the contractor against her.

Cynthia lost the worker's comp trial and was found liable for what amounted to more than $1 million in medical and other costs. Fortunately for her, she was able to force her own company's worker's comp insurance to cover the cost so that she and the company were not directly liable. It hurt her worker's comp rates, but it was better than losing that kind of capital out of her own company.

"I went into a deep depression over the inequity of it all," she said, looking back. "I wasn't given a chance because of the statute. I hated that the relevance of the cocaine test was thrown out. The whole affair severely affected my personal life and my outlook for a long time."

One thing and one thing alone pulled her out of that downward spiral. It was a trait that every successful entrepreneur has: tenacity.

"When my lawyer said I could possibly lose everything, I said 'Fine'. If I lose it all I'll just begin again—sell everything and get over it," Cynthia said. "I'd sell my house and move into a two-bedroom apartment and build it all again from the ground up. There was no way I was going to let this take my dream away from me.

"In the end, I found out I was stronger than I thought. I realized I could persevere. I realized I was smarter than I thought I was. It made me more confident and secure. Believe me, I don't sweat the small stuff anymore," she said.

LOST:

Tens of thousands of dollars in legal and insurance fees, and one-and-a-half years of happiness.

WHAT HAPPENED:

SHE DIDN'T HAVE PROPER PREVENTATIVE PROCESSES IN PLACE.

The biggest problem with the entrepreneur mindset—and there's no real way to correct it—is that entrepreneurs are so enthusiastic and dedicated to their goals and their work that they assume everyone else is as well. It's that optimism that is part and parcel to success. They assume everyone else is going to be as enthusiastic and honest as they are. It's almost unfathomable to the average entrepreneur that someone would do what this contractor did.

Cynthia asked him for his insurance documents. He presented documents on a policy that had expired. Ballsy, to say the least—if someone takes the time to present requested documents and go through a semi-formal process, one's defenses are down at that point.

Cynthia now has in place a formal procedure for background checks on contractors, franchisees, and employees, and one that goes to the source. She doesn't just ask for incorporation papers—she requests documents straight from the secretary of state's office. For insurance and licensing, she ensures policies are active and goes directly to the licensing body for backup.

THE LAW IS NOT ALWAYS YOUR FRIEND.

Cynthia knows law and how to read it. Granted, she's not a labor law expert, but she has a far better grasp on the law than the average Jane or Joe Entrepreneur. Still, it never occurred to her that the statutes in Colorado could have been so stacked against her on this contracting issue. But the fact is, many states have laws in a multitude of areas that are not employer- or business-friendly. For that matter, many states have laws that are not common-sense friendly. Relying on the law to make sense is not the wisest move. When venturing into a new realm, be it geographically or operationally, it's worth the time and expense to have a lawyer check exposure.

There's no way Cynthia could have expected the level of deception that the contractor was willing to engage in, but if she had been told by her lawyer about the liability statute, it's highly likely she would have been more deliberative in her check of the contractor's insurance and bonding status.

QUESTION:

Have you noticed that lack of enough due diligence seems to be a common theme throughout this book? Are you REALLY doing enough due diligence on your customers, suppliers, or contractors to ensure these stories won't happen to you? Never take the promises of key suppliers or contractors at face value—nothing takes the place of thorough due diligence.

SUSAN JONES KNAPE

Susan Knape would seem to have it all—she's successful, smart, attractive—and she was a trailblazer as a woman business owner. In the 1980s, when some women were still trying to reach—much less break through—the glass ceiling, Susan had a mind to go her own way and establish her own advertising and public relations agency.

It didn't happen overnight. The former fashion model, mother of two children, and author of *The Money Rule: 50 Ways Women Can Make More, Save More and Have More,* Susan was a freelance writer and advertising maven in the early '80s whose expertise and talents kept landing her bigger and better projects. The scope of these projects continued to grow to the point that she started having to contract out the work, overseeing designers, writers, and account executives on large-scale ad and public relations campaigns. Finally, it achieved critical mass, and she established a full-service agency with her then-husband.

But right off the bat there was a problem.

"I went into business without knowing how to run a business. I knew everything about advertising and design and how to handle clients, but it didn't occur to me that I needed to know how to run a business from the financial side," Susan said. "When it started, I didn't sit down and think, 'these are the skill sets I need to have.'"

It's hardly politically correct nowadays, but Susan admits she subconsciously assumed her husband could and would handle the finances. She grew up in the 1960s in a very traditional family, and it sort of imprinted on her mind that men naturally could handle the finances, while she could let her talents shine on the creative side of the business.

Unfortunately, she came to find out her husband was even worse at handling money than she was.

"It was an unbelievable assumption I made. I just figured he had those skill sets we needed. If anything, he had less instinct for it than I did," Susan recalled.

Realizing neither of them were financial wizards, Susan notes now she knows what she should have done: jumped in and learned how to run a company's finances on her own.

"As a business owner, that monkey is ultimately on your back," Susan said definitively and in hindsight. "But I naively thought I could still just be running the creative side, so instead of reaching down deep and finding my own ability to learn the numbers, I hired someone to come in and act as a CFO to the agency."

The man she hired, Mark*, was a CPA who had done similar financial management for other advertising and public relations agencies in Dallas.

Susan brought Mark aboard and turned the entire financial operation over to him. Being as he was a CPA, she even canceled her contract with an outside firm, turning over company taxes to Mark as well.

Whether it was denial or willful ignorance, Susan turned a blind eye to the money side of the business over the next two years, even as she was arranging for the acquisition of her company by a larger firm.

"I'd ask him how our finances were and he'd say 'fine' and that was enough for me," Susan said, the self-reproach in her voice and manner quite evident.

With the potential acquisition of Knape and Knape just months away, Mark finally came to her office and came clean. There was a problem. He'd become quite lax in the collection process. Advertising agencies place media ads and buy products on behalf of their clients, they tack on a fee, and bill their clients directly. The agency's vendors expect payment for their services on a timely basis. If the agency pays its vendors on a timely basis but the client doesn't, cash flow goes south. Mark let several invoices to clients go for so long the agency was virtually unable to pay for the media buys and products it purchased on behalf of its clients. Mark decided it was more important to pay the vendors than the IRS, so he started skipping payroll tax payments. The company was now behind $250,000 in back taxes, and the IRS was becoming increasingly threatening.

Never forsake the IRS in favor of other vendors. It's a guarantee that they will come back to haunt you in ways *nothing* else will.

"I fired him immediately and worked out a deal with the company that was acquiring us—Larken, Meader and Scheidell—to roll the back-owed taxes into the cost of the acquisition. That helped get the IRS off of us, but it meant I had to work extra hard after that to make my own incentive numbers and pay the interest owed to LMS," Susan said. "In the end, if you include penalties and interest, it cost me about $350,000."

LOST:

About $350,000.

WHAT HAPPENED:

GUESS WHAT SUSAN DIDN'T DO WHEN SHE HIRED THE CFO?

Perhaps some budding entrepreneur reading this book will get the idea to start a service agency for other entrepreneurs that goes in and looks for the untied shoelaces that so many entrepreneurs leave dangling. That may be a sure thing.

Susan didn't check Mark's references. She has since learned that Mark had a track record of financial mismanagement at all those agencies on his reference list that at one time so impressed her.

"I just figured then I was too busy for details like that," Susan says now, wryly. "Looking back, it may have taken me an hour to make a few calls. Not spending that hour doing my homework cost me $350,000."

KEEP YOUR MIND ON YOUR MONEY AND YOUR MONEY ON YOUR MIND.

Regardless of gender, not a lot of entrepreneurs like dealing with the books. It's a matter of temperament, not gender disparities. Entrepreneurs are visionaries, which rarely goes hand-in-glove with attention to detail. If an entrepreneur wanted to calculate spreadsheets all day, she'd have been an accountant.

But no matter how tempting the allure of having someone lift the burden, an entrepreneur must always keep control of the company finances.

And at the very least—even if an entrepreneur is only taking weekly or monthly financial summaries—one needs to have an outside CPA firm that can verify the numbers of the in-house financial officer. Balance sheets are vast things that can hide serious problems from the untrained eye. An entrepreneur who can't or won't learn the fundamentals needs an outside agency to supply checks and balances.

"You have to be personally involved," Susan says. "It's your company, no one else's. There is no substitute for that."

THE DOWNSIDE OF SUCCESS

That wasn't the only problem Susan dealt with at the time. Concurrent with her IRS woes, there was a real estate issue as well. When she founded Knape & Knape, she had signed a five-year lease. At the time of the signing, she noted that the landlord wanted her to sign a personal guarantee on the lease. Her own lawyer told her this was "a standard clause" and she took that to mean it was okay.

The problem was, despite her tax problem, she sold her business two years into the five-year lease, and went to the landlord.

"I told them I no longer needed the space, and that I wanted to negotiate a release from my remaining three years," Susan said. "They told me no way, that it was a lease guaranteed for five years, and I was bound to pay them whether I needed the space or not."

The landlord's uncompromising position was: Susan owed them $17,000 a month rent for the next three years, regardless, and she was personally liable for the bill.

"I offered to help find a sublease tenant or pay a percentage, but they were unwilling to give an inch," Susan said.

Finally, her legal counsel told her the only way to get out of the lease obligation was to file personal bankruptcy. Susan was loath to do this—she had no other personal debt—but in the position she found herself in, it was the only way out.

LOST:

The time, trouble, added interest payments, and embarrassment of having a personal bankruptcy on her credit report for seven years.

WHAT HAPPENED:

EMPOWER YOURSELF.

Aside from payroll, real estate is the biggest expense most any company has. When dealing with landlords and your own broker, many entrepreneurs end up feeling as if the other two entities are pulling the strings. But in the case of your broker, YOU are the client. In the case of the landlord, YOU are the customer.

Don't be afraid to confront. Ask questions. If you don't understand something, ask questions until you do. Everything in a real estate deal is negotiable. Your broker should be aggressive, not accommodating.

And just because something is "standard," it doesn't make it "acceptable."

"Bottom line is that you have to confront those issues and you have to be willing to walk away from the deal," Susan says. "And this can be harder for women entrepreneurs than men, but you have to find it in yourself to never give up your control or your financial power."

DRESS THE PART.

This is a lesson for men and women, but let's be honest: women want to look their best no matter the circumstance, while men are more likely to care only when there is something at stake.

Susan is convinced that one of the reasons her landlord was so demanding was that when she showed up with hat in hand to ask for a break, she was, as usual, dressed to the nines—all Prada and Chanel. In fact, she had a similar experience with the IRS.

"I was there to plead my financial dire straits, and all they saw was a former Miss Dallas in high fashion and expensive shoes," Susan says. "I think that made them think I was some trust-fund-family girl who was only poor on paper."

When you're in the position of being the pauper, look it. People judge you by your appearance, and you want to look successful when you are trying to be successful. Well, apply that logic backwards—if you're having to go to your creditors or landlord or the IRS to ask for forgiveness, extensions, or help, think plain Jane.

The most important lesson Susan learned, though?

She sees it as applying more to women, but in truth there's no one who can't benefit from this perspective she has gained.

"Hardships prove character. You have to look at them and learn from them and move on. Things do happen for a reason, and character is being able to take a hardship and turn it to your gain."

QUESTION:

If you don't have a business background, have you taken an accounting and/or finance course that will allow you to have a basic understanding of your company's financial statements?

When signing a legal document, do you have complete knowledge of the repercussions should you have to default?

Are you dressing for the part—up or down?

Name changed for confidentiality.

HAL BRIERLEY

NAME: HAL BRIERLEY

COMPANY: EPSILON DATA MANAGEMENT

INDUSTRY: DATABASE MARKETING

ANNUAL REVENUES: $50 MILLION

It's been said before—in this very book—that clichés get to be clichés for a reason. They are time-tested and true, irreducible axioms such as, Don't judge a book by its cover. Appearances can be deceiving. Or even the more recent Russian proverb, Trust, but verify. And yet, time and again, it seems the best among entrepreneurs still don't heed those old truths.

Hal Brierley is nobody's fool. An engineer by education and an entrepreneur by nature, Hal saw in 1970 the success a fledgling company called Electronic Data Systems was having in systems management, and he determined to carve out his own niche in the field. Partnering with a Harvard Business School classmate, he co-founded Epsilon Data Management (EDM) and focused his attention on nonprofits like the world-famous San Diego Zoo, the World Wildlife Fund, and the U.S. Ski Team.

As is the case with most entrepreneurs, Hal had to be a jack-of-all-trades to get his business off the ground, and he knew his own limits, one of which was accounting. Initially he set up a single-entry set of financial records, which—let's give credit where credit is due—is more than some entrepreneurs can do on their own; they are vision folk, not detail folk.

As the company started to grow, Hal knew he needed additional capital to fund expansion and operations. And going to bankers or venture capitalists with single-digit books wasn't going to cut the mustard.

"I wanted to impress the bankers with a big-name CPA firm, so we brought in [what was then] Price Waterhouse to perform the audit for the year-end," Hal said. "It was during that audit I met Kenneth*, a young hotshot who impressed me with both his presentation and his schooling."

Delegation, of course, is a key to success, and Hal knew it. After all, his very business concept—outsourced data management—was based on the idea of delegation and focusing on core competencies.

"I decided to hire Kenneth, bringing him in as controller, so I could turn my attention to sales and growing the company," Hal said.

With Kenneth on board, Hal focused on growing the company further. He was not disappointed. Over the course of the next few years, things couldn't go wrong, it seemed. Kenneth submitted to Hal monthly financial reports that showed fast internal growth and solid black ink. In fact, all the pretty numbers looked so good that in December 1973, Hal was able to secure an additional $200,000 in venture capital to fund even more growth.

The EDM ship seemed to be sailing at full steam with nothing but open water as far as the eye could see. But in actuality, the EDM ship's hull was leaking, and there were dire straits ahead.

In the spring of 1974, EDM had grown to the extent that Hal felt he needed to hire a vice president of finance administration, some-one Kenneth would report to. When the new VP came on board, Kenneth quit. This should have set off red alert klaxons, but things had seemed to be going so well that, while the resignation was disappointing and puzzling, no one assumed the worst.

"When we moved in to pick up the reins, we found an incredible mess in Kenneth's office, and I'm not talking about the décor," Hal said, with some disgust still evident more than twenty-five years after the incident.

All those pretty numbers and monthly financial reports, it turns out, were a sham. Hal found stack after stack of unprocessed bills. Expenses were listed as assets. What seemed an even shade of black ink transformed into an angry torrent of red ink as bloody as a Stephen King nightmare. In a day, the company went from financially sound and awash in capital to cast adrift and sinking fast.

"It was so bad that after three days of wading through stacks of papers that Kenneth left behind, the new VP quit," Hal said.

Hal and his existing team faced an ugly fact—they were going to have to work it out themselves. The saving grace was that while Kenneth was busy playing three-card monte with the company's financials, Hal had not wasted that free time. He had acquired a slate of new business, the billings for which kept the company solvent over the course of the next year. It took severe belt-tightening, personal attention to creditors, and ensuring that commitments were kept across the board to maintain the company's solvency and image. There was no magic trick to undoing the damage that was done—it took old-fashioned elbow grease and gumption. By 1978, the company was back in the black, posting 10 percent net profit on revenues of $10 million.

LOST:

One year of what could have been growth; endless late nights; nearly a whole business.

WHAT HAPPENED:

IGNORANCE IS NOT BLISS.

Have you noticed a compelling but very common theme throughout this book? It's the very nature of the entrepreneur that is his or her biggest weakness. *Few focus on the details.* Most are eternal optimists about life and human nature, and thus they often hear only what they want to hear. Many are impressed by a highfalutin' degree in a subject they don't understand much about. Entrepreneurs hold as their highest value their honesty to the vision they create—whatever the product or service—so the very idea of someone acting under false pretenses is anathema to their nature. Sure, they know intellectually that frauds exist and that people can lie, but detecting it is just not in their instincts.

"You can't be out of touch with things critical to your business—that's not what delegation is about. You may give over the responsibility for the work, but what you don't give over is the responsibility for the outcome," Hal said. "That always rests on your shoulders."

The lessons Hal learned from EDM have come in handy for him as he is now the founder and Chief Loyalty Architect of Brierley and Partners, a 200-employee firm specializing in customer relationship management.

QUESTION:

Have you let yourself get out of touch with a critical function of your business? Being the boss may mean having the perks of not having to do the grunt work, but it always falls on your shoulders and your bottom line if that grunt work is not done right.

Have you hired someone to fill a function you don't understand? Then have a system for cross-checking—even CPAs have other CPAs audit their books—and trust your instincts if something seems odd or too good to be true. Better to ask a "stupid question" than to make a stupid move.

* Name changed for confidentiality.

LARRY WINGET

NAME: LARRY WINGET

COMPANY: ADTEL, INC.

INDUSTRY: TELECOMMUNICATIONS

ANNUAL REVENUES: $2 MILLION

Don't come to Larry Winget with sob stories. As one of the highest-paid non-celebrity professional speakers in America, with nineteen books under his belt, Larry won't sugarcoat it.

"Suck it up and get back on the track."

Today Larry is known as the pit bull of motivational speakers. He is a philosopher of success who just happens to be hilarious. He teaches universal principles that work for anyone in any business at any time, and he does it through simple examples, understandable, easy-to-implement ideas, and funny stories.

He teaches that business improves when the people in the business improve, and that everything in life gets better when we get better and nothing gets better until we get better. And he doesn't believe in feeling sorry for yourself.

It's an attitude that has served him well. In the 1980s he took his telecommunications company to the top, then lost it all. Everything. Down to nearly the last brick of his house.

It is an odd trail Larry has traveled. A typical small-town boy who grew up on a chicken ranch in Muskogee, Oklahoma, Larry started out as (in his words) poor white trash.

After getting his college degrees in psychology and library science (yes, really!), he went to work for Southwestern Bell as one of their first male operators. Showing a remarkable aptitude for selling to people, he naturally worked into sales and marketing, eventually becoming area sales manager for Kansas for AT&T.

When the company underwent divestiture in the early 1980s, Larry was one of the first out the door, with a year's salary severance, an absolute faith he could sell anything to anyone, and absolutely no idea how to start and run a business.

But then that's the thing about Larry—he is not a detail person, and that unyielding faith in himself wasn't about to let a detail like no experience slow him down. He moved to Tulsa, Oklahoma, and started his own business telecommunications company.

"I knew nothing about going into business, but I had one skill," Larry says, his laid-back southwestern accent unapologetic, his tone quietly confident. "I knew I could sell stuff better than anyone. So I found a guy who was an installer, and pretty soon we had more installations than he could handle. So we kept hiring more and more people. In a very short couple of years, we built the largest independent telecommunications company in Oklahoma."

Larry approached the business the way he did everything else: confidently and not sweating the details. Like many other entrepreneurs, he was and is a leader, not a manager. He was bored by figures and forms, and he wasn't the kind who could sit behind a desk all day.

He did keep his eye on the big picture and the bottom line, but he had a straightforward, salesman's solution for dealing with things when cash flow and income got tight—he would just increase revenues. More sales. And he got them.

Then, after several years of solid growth, Larry just lost interest. Telecommunications no longer captivated him, if it ever had.

"I knew I wanted to be a speaker. I just wanted a stage and an audience, and I'd be happy," Larry said.

So, after not much deliberation, Larry set his course. He put what he believed to be good managers in charge of his company, and he left them to run it while he went out to learn the speaking trade. Sounds like a reasonable solution—hold onto the current success while pursuing a new one. The company was grossing $2 million in annual sales and still growing strong. So what could go wrong?

There may be tales of faster collapses in the business world, but it's a hard search to find them.

"I never was good with numbers, and I wasn't interested in them," he said. "So I didn't notice how sales were dropping and expenses mounting."

"Literally, within months they ran the company into the ground," he said. "I never focused too much on the details when I was there, but to the degree I did, combined with good managers following my lead, that's how we prospered. Without that direction, the company basically imploded."

Complicating matters, the "good managers" he thought he had running the company also failed to pay payroll taxes for about a year. He came back into the company and tried to set things right, but the momentum of failure had already reached terminal velocity. The only course was bankruptcy. He filed in 1989.

"Overspending and overextending did us in. We were victims of our own successes," he said. "I lost everything. Everything. And I was in debt to the IRS. It was horrible. I was afraid to pick up the phone. Afraid I'd lose my house. I even sold my gold Rolex to make a house payment. I had a garage sale every weekend."

The careful reader knows this was hardly the end. In fact, for Larry, his failure was the beginning of his real success.

"I realized that ten years before I had started out with nothing, so I said to myself, 'I can do it again,'" Larry says. "In retrospect, I'm glad it all happened. I wouldn't be where I am today if it hadn't happened. That's what got me motivated to go out and read a couple thousand books and learn everything I could about being a professional speaker, because that's all I ever wanted to do."

His first step: selling what he already knew—his sales knowledge. He broke out the Tulsa Yellow Pages and called every business in the book. Whether they had one person or one hundred in sales, he asked to train them.

"I charged as little as $50 for three hours, and if it was just one salesperson and me, I was there," he says.

Within a couple of months, Larry attended the opening of the Oklahoma Speakers Association—borrowing $25 from his household food fund, no less—and went to get advice from other professionals.

"They said it took five or six years to be in this business before you could really make a living at it. I had five or six weeks to start making money. And I had a lifestyle I wasn't willing to sacrifice much longer."

So, again, not worrying about details like having no real experience, Larry got on the phone. And he worked. And worked. And worked. In thirty-seven days, Larry had booked for himself $85,000 worth of business—and that was back when his fee was as little as $1,200 a shot.

He hasn't looked back. Today, he travels as many as three hundred days a year, speaking for one of the highest rates of pay in the business.

"What kept me going strong was that I never questioned my ability to succeed. And I didn't just set out to be a speaker—I set out to be the best, richest, most well-known speaker in the business," Larry said. "I believe you can force success, but what it takes is a willingness to force it. No half measures, no compromises."

LOST:

Tens of millions. An entire successful, independent telecommunications company. And remember, this was before the telecommunications boom of the 1990s.

WHAT HAPPENED:

KEEP YOUR EYES ON THE ROAD AND THE GAUGES.

Entrepreneurs do what they do in part because they cannot march to the beat of other drummers. They are often big-picture people. But if they can't force themselves to examine their own blind spots, they need people they know can pay attention to those details.

Larry hates numbers. He needed people who could watch those details for him. He thought he had them—he didn't. If an entrepreneur can't do his own due diligence on some area of the business, that entrepreneur darn well better do due diligence on the person hired to watch those details. Have an accountability process in place. Blind trust is a good way to get run down.

"It was my fault—my company. I should have been paying attention. I had no accountability process in place. And in turn, the managers I had didn't have any sense of ownership in the company, so naturally they weren't as careful as I would have been."

AS YOU CHASE SUCCESS, BE WARY OF SUCCESS.

Success can be an entrepreneur's biggest enemy. It can make you lazy. It can make you stop paying attention to the little stuff—the details that garnered that share of success in the first place.

"Success is a dangerous thing. We made too much money too fast and spent too much too quickly."

LOVE IT OR LEAVE IT.

Do you love the business you are in? If not, consider selling it or officially getting out. Keeping ownership in a venture you are not adequately overseeing can be a formula for liability problems. You may be thinking, "They do the work, I keep the profits," and that can sometimes be true. But it also means, "They run the business into the ground, I keep all the debts."

"No one will take care of a business like it's yours. If you want out, get out clean."

DON'T LISTEN TO "CAN'T"; DO WHAT IT TAKES.

A fool doesn't listen to the lessons of others, but a bigger fool is the one who lets the experience of others mark his or her limits. Learn from other trail riders, but don't hesitate to blaze your own trail.

Larry wasn't willing to listen to those who told him he would be at it for years before he could make a living. He just got to work.

"Most people lack willingness to learn and to do what they need to succeed. I was willing to go speak to ten sleepy old men in the basement of a church for their Kiwanis Club, because I wanted to get podium time to learn and sharpen what I did. That's why I am where I am."

QUESTION:

Are you thinking about starting an additional business while keeping your existing one? If you plan to hand over day-to-day management responsibility to an employee of your current company, do you have a solid accountability plan in place which includes a strict reporting schedule AND your continued involvement?

Are you willing to do whatever you must do to see yourself succeed, or is it not that important to you?

Section Six

Tough Times

Jo Ann Brumit

Jo Ann Brumit didn't take the usual road to business success. The daughter of an entrepreneur, she got a slow start out of the gates on her way to entrepreneurship, getting married and having children right out of high school. She wasn't just a stay-at-home mom though. She went to work for a small company that encouraged her to go to night school to learn accounting.

"As close as I came to ever owning a company at that point was serving as a sort of quasi-controller," Jo Ann said.

After having her second child, unfortunately, as is often (though not always) the case with high school romances, the marriage ended in divorce.

"My dad had always preached to me that the only way to really be happy and control your own life is to own your own business. I didn't start my career that way, but I eventually came to it," she said.

Jo Ann got to work building her business skills, taking more classes and seminars on accounting, business administration, and finance. One of those extension seminars brought her to Dallas, where she met a man who had a small gas company with about fourteen employees.

"At the seminar, he told me it took three women to do his payroll, and he asked me to see if I could help resolve that problem," Jo Ann said. "I came on as a consultant, and after I streamlined the operations, we no longer had three people doing the work of one."

The owner of the then-small oil company, KARLEE, was so impressed he wanted to hire Jo Ann full time.

"Remembering what my dad said, I told him I would do it, but I would have to own a part of the business or I wouldn't come aboard. He said, 'Sure,'" Jo Ann recalled.

The worst you can get when you ask is a no. Be bold.

The owner was impressed with her moxie, more so than either realized at the time, because over the course of the next year, a romance blossomed. About a year later, he asked Jo Ann to marry him. During the next twenty years, Jo Ann and her husband—and later joining them their children—built the company into a large business boasting $80 million in annual sales and more than five hundred employees.

Jo Ann's vision was to create a manufacturing organization focused on customer service, producing customer-specified products through the best processes available while building the most knowledgeable team in the industry. The company evolved from oil and gas to becoming a provider of customized integrated manufacturing services such as sheet metal fabrication, precision machining, cabling, electromechanical assembly, and process coating. In the late 1990s, the company focused on the semiconductor and telecommunications industries as a customer base.

So successful was their operation that in 2000, the company was honored with the highly prestigious national Malcolm Baldrige Award, recognizing performance, profitability, and excellence.

That year the company executives were invited to the White House to be recognized. As it was a transition year, President Bill Clinton invited KARLEE to the Oval Office, but President George W. Bush actually presented the award in 2001.

Just when things looked as if they couldn't get any better, the other shoe dropped.

"We were coming off this tremendous high—our best year ever. In six months our sales started falling off. We held on and on until finally we realized we'd have to do layoffs, and we did it a lot later than we should have—by at least six months," Jo Ann said. "We had to cut our workforce from 500 to 185 within a year, and this is a company that had never laid off anyone. We had experienced positive revenue and profit growth every year since 1980. The run rate on revenue went from $80 million to $12 million. Most companies don't survive that.

"We simply weren't prepared for anything like that. We weren't diversified. I personally didn't really know much about capital raising. We were 85 percent concentrated in telecom, and when that industry went bust, we not only saw a loss in our orders, but we had companies unable to pay for product they already had ordered," Jo Ann said. "I had kept the company well diversified until the mid-1990s in Dallas when telecom skyrocketed, and I didn't want to miss out on that opportunity."

No matter how tempting the payoff, never put all your eggs in one basket. It may be smart to think your margin would be greater if more of your business was invested in industry X, but if industry X goes bye-bye, so will your business. Diversify, no matter what.

"We also just didn't react fast enough. As painful as it may be, it's better to cut sooner—people or equipment—rather than later, because cash reserve is more critical than anything," she said.

You can't just tread water, which is what Jo Ann tried to do. One way or the other you have to move—downsize, rightsize, cut costs, move ahead, whatever—if you stay still you will eventually tire out, sink, and drown.

Jo Ann went to her capital partners and her banker, telling them that she needed help to recover—extensions, new loans, additional funding—only to have them shut the door in her face.

"I made the grand mistake of having only one banker. I had no power and no leverage. They had me over a barrel," she said.

It's been said time and again, having options is having power. And it's during the good times that you should prepare for the bad. Opening avenues to access capital is easier when skies are blue and the money is pouring in. When you go hat-in-hand looking for capital and trouble is following you, that's when you'll find yourself hearing, "No."

These days, Jo Ann has set up a process whereby they keep a close eye on revenue and costs and they have a set formula of what the ratio needs to be. If that ratio is not met, no matter how close it is shaved, they will cut expenses immediately.

"We have to take care of the whole. In the case of personnel, as much as it may pain us and as much as we'd like to take care of everyone, we have come to accept that sometimes you have to sacrifice an individual for the whole," she said.

When income falls, cut expenses wherever you can. You can always bring them back into play when you recover, but your cash flow is your life's blood.

The road to recovery was hard fought, and they are still rebuilding. They put a lot of focus into sales in a wider range of industries. And they approached the employee issue the only way they thought would be right—with candor and honesty.

"We are very honest and straightforward with our employees. We tell them 'Here is where we are, and we may have to lay off X number, but not for two weeks at least. You focus on your job and meeting customer needs. If we don't we'll have to cut more. But if we do right, we will retain the customer and thus our people.' They appreciate that we are in a tough time, and that we are being straight with them," Jo Ann said. "Because of this, despite the uncertainty, they give us their best, knowing that we are fighting to keep them aboard. They have an investment in the company."

Honesty and conveying a sense of proprietary ownership will get you more from your people than any other approach.

KARLEE posted $19 million in revenue in 2003 and is on track to achieve $28 million in sales for 2004. All the processes are coming back into place, and they are building back that momentum that carried them forward.

Jo Ann did gain one other lesson. Though she has turned the business around, she was reminded that at the end of the day, her own well-being and sense of self were not entirely attached to the business she owned.

"The whole experience really tested my faith. At first, it was difficult to just get through a day. But as the days turned into weeks, I realized that I would be okay even if KARLEE failed. For twenty-plus years I linked my success to KARLEE. I thought my purpose was to grow KARLEE, touching the lives of those who came into contact with KARLEE," she said. "I realize now that God has the plan and I need to just walk through each day in faith and be open and ready for each door that might open. It is amazing how much less you worry and how much more confident you feel to tackle the unknown when you come to that place.

"It was also amazing to watch the support and willingness of the KARLEE team members to come together and even take pay cuts to ensure the survival of KARLEE," she said. "KARLEE is stronger and more focused on bottom-line performance today. We are a more diversified company and understand our weaknesses better."

LOST:

Millions in revenue. An unbroken track record of revenue growth. Some false illusions.

WHAT HAPPENED:

BEING READY FOR NOW ISN'T ENOUGH.

The road will get rocky. Those things you factor into your success equation as constants are variables, subject to change as surely as everything else in life. It's not enough to be on top of what is happening now. Contingency plans have to be in place for every possible eventuality—loss of revenue streams, changes in the markets for your goods or services, changes in the needs of your clients. Work it out ahead of time with your capital resources alternatives, in case things go awry.

In short, no matter what the issue, you should, as is a constant theme in this book, always, always have options.

QUESTION:

Is your customer base diversified? If not, are you keeping current on the health of the industry in which you specialize?

No one predicted the rapid decline of the telecommunications industry, but that decline destroyed many, many businesses. Spreading your revenue sources over as many different organizations and industries as possible will minimize risk and make your company more attractive should you ever search for new money or a potential buyer.

Rob Solomon

NAME: ROB SOLOMON

COMPANY: US ONLINE HOLDINGS, INC.

INDUSTRY: TELECOMMUNICATIONS

ANNUAL REVENUES: $40 MILLION

> If you can make one heap of all your winnings
> and risk it on one turn of pitch and toss,
> and lose and start again at your beginnings
> and never breathe a word about your loss . . .
> ■ *"If" by Rudyard Kipling*

We're going to stray away from the tactical lessons in this chapter. We're going to look at things a little more holistically and philosophically. Rob Solomon's story is like many others—he's the first to say that sometimes he thinks his story is a bit clichéd in the world of business mistakes. What's unique is the time he spent after his crash focusing on the lessons he could take away from it. Sometimes, no matter how good, smart, savvy, wise, or prepared you are, you can't snatch victory from the jaws of defeat.

But how we handle ourselves in defeat is at least as important as how we work toward our success. So in this chapter, instead of focusing on the specifics of where Rob made his mistakes, we'd like to focus on the bigger-picture lessons Rob learned as a result of crashing into the wall.

Rob is in many ways your typical entrepreneur, in that he worked his way through college. His first job was as a partner in a start-up real estate venture. Barely a year into the venture, Rob started his own multifamily real estate investment, management, and development firm, focusing on properties in Texas.

In 1996, Rob fell into the telecommunications industry almost by accident. A dispute with a cable provider for one of his multifamily properties in San Antonio ended with his firm building its own small cable system for the property. Very rapidly, he expanded this venture to his other multifamily properties, eventually spinning off the enterprise as US Online. In no time at all, US Online was seeking out other large multifamily properties, wiring them for long distance, local, cable, and Internet access.

This was the heyday of consumer-level telecommunications—the world was getting wired.

"We started with no employees, no customers, and no revenues. Within three years we were operating in nine cities; we had revenues around $40 million; over 100 employees; we were public with market cap of about $100 million," Rob said. "We were on a hot sales trajectory and in the best space we could be in at the time—technology and telecommunications. The world had gone crazy on revenue growth instead of profit, and subscribership rather than income was paramount."

It was a heady time.

"In telecom you have to choose between growth and profitability. If you want to grow, you have to put a lot of money into it," Rob said. "We became like heroin addicts—we couldn't spend or build fast enough to keep up with our demand."

Complicating it all was the complexity of the telecommunications industry itself, especially for someone like Rob, who admits he is no technologist.

"It's a business with a lot of moving parts—technology, regulations, dynamics specific to multifamily communities, and the capital component," he said.

To feed the growth beast, Rob had to seek several rounds of outside funding. He spent a lot of time—a year, in fact—focused solely on his business and on seeking capital. He figures he racked up 200,000 frequent flier miles, missed several family birthdays, and put a serious strain on his marriage. Twice when he thought he had secured venture capital funding, the rug was pulled out from under him at the last moment, through last second revaluations or ratchcting term changes.

After a year wasted chasing the dragon, Rob considered taking the company public, but it was the end of 1998 and the Russell 2000 had just gone belly-up—meaning it was well nigh impossible for a small-cap telecom firm to effectively place an IPO. No reason to give up though—with some outside advice, Rob figured he should do a reverse merger with a publicly-traded company, and he did.

"Once we realized that this was the best route for us to go public, we raised the equity we needed to make the deal happen," Rob said. "We secured almost $100 million in new capital."

But just as soon as things came together, they began to fall apart. For one, Rob suddenly realized he was no longer the primary decision maker in his own company.

"I went from being in a company I owned and controlled to being in a company where I was an employee with a big equity stake. It became a democracy—instead of making decisions myself, there was a lot of rule by committee. I had to answer to shareholders and outside board," Rob said. "The stress of that got exacerbated by the way the industry went from boom to bust so quickly."

In the course of the next year—1999–2000—the telecommunications and tech industry bubble burst. Everyone got whacked. The giants and the little guys fell apart seemingly overnight.

"That massive sucking sound was capital markets pulling out of telecom," Rob said. "Valuations went from being subscriber-based to revenue-based. Good and bad companies got caught up and went down. That was the scene. It was ugly."

This is where we skip the details in this particular story—suffice it to say Rob's relationship with the board of directors started getting worse, he eventually got out, and not long after, the company went virtually belly-up. It's still in business, but in a no-growth mode, barely a fraction of its former late-1990s glory.

What's important in this story is the aftermath.

"I spent a lot of time being retrospective about the whole experience," Rob said. "I didn't bog myself down in being depressed about seeing a $40 million business crash—I tried to focus on the good I could take from it. I thought back about how much

I had learned about capital markets, about people, about technology, about dealing with government regulations, and about money.

"More important, I thought about how I had taken on a Superman complex, and how that necessary dose of humility brought me back down to earth," he said. "I learned that I couldn't try to lord over things I don't really understand—the technology or the government regulations. I tried to control all of that even though none of it was in my area of expertise.

"I also learned that from start to finish, I never really had a goal with US Online. I didn't have what they call a B.H.A.G.—a Big Hairy Audacious Goal," Rob said. "What was the point of running a successful business if I didn't even know what the end goal was?"

In the end, Rob said, he gained clarity of vision. He learned a lesson that's hard for Type A personalities to accept—that there are going to be some things you can't control, and that you have to be humble enough to know there are things you don't know.

"At US Online, I found myself reacting to things I couldn't change, and that was a waste. One of my life lessons is that it doesn't work for me to be in a position where I'm just reacting and not in control," he said. "I focus now on businesses I can understand and control. I don't get in businesses that require a lot of money, people, or government interference. I'm mercenary about that. 'Keep it simple' is my rule.

"I also surround myself with people who are smarter than I am. I don't try to be a strategist in places where I'm not qualified to be one," Rob said. "And most important, after nearly ruining my health and my relationships with my obsession about my business,

I have found the need for balance in my life, my work, my marriage, and my health."

Today, Rob resides in Austin, Texas, with his wife, Tracy, and two sons. A serial entrepreneur, he applies the lessons from the US Online fiasco to achieve a golden mean of success in all aspects of his life. He is currently the principal of Bulldog Solutions, which provides conferencing solutions, including audio, Web, and videoconferencing platforms, to small, medium, and large businesses throughout the U.S. and Canada. He also serves as CEO of Keedo USA, a distributor for an African designer clothing line. In addition, he leads an investment group that acquired and now runs the Texas Sailing Academy, one of the oldest U.S. Coast Guard-certified sailing academies in the United States, providing instruction, charter, maintenance and repair, and brokerage services.

LOST:

A $40 million company.

GAINED:

A life.

QUESTION:

Are you prepared, mentally and spiritually, for the day circumstances beyond your control may dash your venture against the rocky shoals?

Do you have it in you to pick up the pieces and carry on, and not miss the lessons even a failure can teach you?

MERLE VOLDING

NAME: MERLE VOLDING

COMPANY: BANCTEC INC.

INDUSTRY: HIGH-TECH PROCESSING SYSTEMS FOR BANKS

ANNUAL REVENUES: $600 MILLION

This is a short story that focuses on how sometimes you have to go against both conventional wisdom and sound practices—and even some of the lessons you'll find in this book.

Eighty years old and still snow-skiing and hiking, Merle Volding's résumé reads like a highlight of some of the most pivotal moments in history. Not even out of his teens, Merle was serving in the Pacific theater of operations in World War II as a cryptographer. He was an accountant and controller for some of the Dallas area's most important companies in the 1950s. In the golden age of IBM, from the late 1950s through the 1960s, he was a programmer, manager, marketer, and salesman for Big Blue. And after a stint as executive vice president for a different $200 million company, in 1971—at an age when some professionals are considering early retirement—Merle founded his own company, BancTec.

Not too shabby for a man born on an Iowa farm, whose formal schooling consisted of using the GI Bill to attain an accounting degree from the University of Iowa. But, as we see with entrepreneurs, their accomplishments are stepping-stones on a lifelong journey rather than ends in themselves.

After decades as a company man, Merle said he got his first real grounding in the entrepreneurial experience by serving as an executive vice president for Recognition Equipment, Inc. He wasn't the founder, but he was with it from near its inception to its growth to a $200 million company. But as the company grew, and even as he learned lessons in the entrepreneurial experience, he became disenchanted with the way the firm was run. So he struck out on his own to form BancTec, which focused on developing high-tech processing systems for banks and credit card companies, ranging from smaller items that encoded checks, to larger, high-speed image processors.

From 1971 through the early 1980s, BancTec grew to about a $40 million company, largely because of the smaller technology items. But the goal was to develop and sell larger, integrated processing systems, such as what evolved into the multimillion-dollar IMPAC system.

It was 1983, and the company had just sold its first IMPAC system to Citibank South Dakota, when the national economy took a downturn.

"When the economy is bad, it's hard to get big corporations to invest in multimillion-dollar big-ticket items being sold by smaller companies. In their minds, the risk increases exponentially," Merle said.

Developing and refining the IMPAC system was a costly, ongoing expense for BancTec, and with deals that were on the table stalling out, the company quickly went from seven-figure profits (in 1983 dollars) to seven-figure deficits.

"We had a meeting of the board on how far we could cut back, and we even discussed cutting product development because it was so costly—but I was against that because it would be throwing in the towel," he said.

Cuts were made everywhere they could find fat. Hard decisions were made—including letting employees go. Merle himself realized that to close the deals that were in limbo, he had to get out on the road and help close them.

"When a small firm is selling a big-ticket item to big companies like Citibank and American Express, they like to meet with the CEO directly instead of just a salesman," he said.

But that meant he couldn't devote any of his time to overseeing operations. Fortunately, Merle knew a financial expert from his days at Recognition Equipment whom he could trust implicitly. Merle got out and sold, and he hired his trusted financial expert to run the operations.

With hard work, elbow grease, painful cuts, and by throwing himself entirely into sales, Merle and his team pulled the company out of its rut. With the economy booming again by 1987, he retired from management of the firm, but remained on the board until 1994.

LOST:

Nearly a company.

WHAT HAPPENED:

NOTHING MERLE COULD CONTROL BUT THINGS HE COULD FIX.

Economic downs are part of life, and every entrepreneurial venture is a risk. Merle took some drastic steps and saved his company, and along the way he learned some valuable lessons.

IN CASE OF EMERGENCY, BREAK THE RULES.

Time and again in this book, we warn that no one will take care of your company like you will, and that you can't afford to overlook anything. But there may come a time, as it did for Merle, when the only way to deal with a critical problem is focusing your all on it—even if it's to the exclusion of your regular duties. Merle was fortunate in that he knew a man he trusted personally and who was an excellent operations executive.

LISTEN TO THE CYNICS—HIRE YOUR OWN, IN FACT.

Optimism is the entrepreneur's best friend and greatest fuel. It's also the entrepreneur's Achilles' heel. Without going into detail, Merle said there were several signs that trouble was brewing in 1983, but he was just sure the deals would close and things would continue on track.

"I didn't have anything to balance my optimism," he says.

Don't be afraid to have a devil's advocate on your team. Encourage an atmosphere where your executives will be more than just "yes" people. You may not—and you don't have to—agree with them, but they serve to make you think about points they bring up. If you have someone you really trust on your leadership team, encourage him to meet with you behind closed doors and actively take the role of naysayer, even if he doesn't endorse the negative view. It's a tool that strengthens what you're doing right and can help you foresee that which you might do wrong, and thus you can change course before it becomes an issue.

QUESTION:

If your primary cash flow were staunched tomorrow, do you have other sources of recurring revenue in value-added services or maintenance you can perform for existing clients?

Do you have someone who has earned the trust to take over some of your duties, should you be forced to turn your attention to a single aspect of your business?

Do you have the courage and will to make the kind of cuts needed to ensure your business weathers a financial storm?

DR. ROSEMARY ROSETTI

NAME: DR. ROSEMARY ROSETTI, PHD

COMPANY: ROSETTI ENTERPRISES

INDUSTRY: CONSULTANT, AUTHOR, SPEAKER

ANNUAL REVENUES: NOT AVAILABLE

Rosemary Rosetti's story is unique in this book—the challenge she faced in her business was not one of marketing, finance, operations, personnel, partners, or legalities. It was not the result of a failure or mistake of her making, or of others'. It was not a market downturn.

It was, quite literally, an act of God.

So why is this story here? As Rosemary so aptly puts it—an entrepreneur is her business, and her business is her life.

Entrepreneurs are on their own—they don't have "the company" to rely on. As the thought leader in their enterprises, they are often the irreplaceable component; they are the engines pulling the train. Regardless of his or her business model, market, or industry, an entrepreneur needs to have contingencies in place.

It was 1998, one year after Rosemary had left her teaching position at Ohio State University to become a professional trainer, speaker, writer, and business consultant. In fact, the former agricultural education professor, design horticulturalist, and co-author of *The Healthy Indoor Plant,* a gardening instruction book, remembers the day as vividly as if it were moments ago. Were it part of a Hollywood screenplay, it might be considered too tragically coincidental.

It was her third wedding anniversary, June 13. She and her husband, Mark, decided to celebrate that afternoon with a bike ride just outside Columbus, Ohio. They drove to a trail on that gorgeous sunny day.

"When we got there, we took the bikes off the car, and that's when I took my last step. It was a beautiful day, a Caribbean blue sky, and the weather was perfect. We pretty much had the trail to ourselves," she recounted. "We were on our way for an ice cream cone at the end of the ride."

She heard her husband say, "Look over there, something is falling." She saw a few leaves falling—this in the middle of summer—and some instinct told her to speed up. Mark yelled, "Look out!" but it was too late. She never saw it coming.

An eighty-foot tree fell onto the trail, crushing Rosemary. In a split second her life was changed—five vertebrae in her back and two in her neck were crushed. She was paralyzed from the waist down.

After extensive surgery, including bone transplants from her hip to her back, Rosemary spent five days in intensive care followed by five weeks in the hospital in rehabilitation.

At that time she owned two companies—a publishing company and a speaking, training, and consulting firm. But in her own words, "With that kind of injury, you're out of commission. I'm fortunate I had disability income insurance. It became my life support system so that financially I wasn't ruined."

A friend and fellow speaker, Randall Reader, came to visit her every day in the hospital—he even sent out a daily e-mail to her friends about her condition. When she finally got out of the hospital, Rosemary would spend two more years going back three days a week for occupational and rehabilitation therapy.

Many people, even the most driven entrepreneurs, might throw up their hands and resign themselves to a diminished life, at most. Not Rosemary, and not her friend Randall. He insisted she partner with him on a speaking assignment just two months after she was out of the hospital. She thinks it's ironic that the subject of the seminar was "How to Get Over Your Fear of Public Speaking"—since she was dealing with her first time speaking on stage in a wheelchair.

It wasn't easy. She couldn't fulfill all the bookings she'd made prior to her accident. Rosemary had the foresight to have plans in place with fellow speakers, people who could step in for her and vice versa, should the need arise. But she didn't have the communication management infrastructure in place, and in those early weeks she wasn't entirely lucid due to the pain medications. Back then, she kept her appointments and contacts in an old Franklin planner. Her husband tried his best to figure out her system, but it wasn't easy.

With help and hard work, she did work through it all, but too many calls went unanswered, and too many things didn't get done. As will be revealed, a proper plan in place could have circumvented those troubles.

Rosemary was also fortunate she had the foresight to have both health and disability income insurance. Seems a little obvious, but entrepreneurs often cut their personal expenses to the bone when they are first starting out.

"People should look at their insurance and make sure they have coverage for the worst-case scenario," she said.

Rosemary lived through an event that could have ended her life—first literally, and then later metaphorically. Her own tenacity, ethics, ambition, and dogged determination got her through the physical threat. That same ambition helped her continue and then transform her business.

Today, her successful business focuses on motivational speaking in addition to the training and consulting. Her writing has expanded beyond the subject of horticulture to the vibrant story of the life she has built after the accident. She is a published columnist as well. But it's doubtful she could have made it on will alone. Rosemary had some plans in place—maybe not everything, but enough. In hindsight she wishes she had more extensive coverage.

Every entrepreneur is the all-seeing god of his or her own universe. The irreducible primary standing above the composite mass. The shepherd who stands over the sheepdogs and the sheep. This is a given: absolute belief in oneself is critical to the entrepreneurial mindset; otherwise the entrepreneur would be someone else's employee. Entrepreneurs lead.

But sometimes, like Julius Caesar receiving accolades from the senate, the entrepreneur needs someone to walk alongside her, whispering in her ear the reminder, "Thou art mortal."

Things can happen to take a leader out of the picture temporarily. The smart entrepreneur has contingencies in place to ensure money flow, to facilitate communications, to take the reins until she can step back in. Be it personal or business related, the wise work toward the best, but are prepared for the worst.

It's okay to carry the world on your shoulders. Just be sure to have somewhere to place it and keep it safe if you are forced to shrug for a moment or two.

QUESTION:

What do you think the chances are of being paralyzed by a falling tree? Virtually impossible? So thought Rosemary. Do you have contingency plans in place for your personal and business assets? Are your contacts and contracts set up in such a way that someone could take over for you? Do you have adequate disability insurance in case a catastrophe such as this strikes you?

Section Seven

Selling Your "Baby"

JEFF STEPLER

Jeff Stepler could relate like few other people to Michael Corleone's angry lament in *The Godfather III*. "Just when I think I'm out, they keep pulling me back in!"

Canadian by birth and with a knack for teaching, Jeff got started in the field of creating courseware in 1989 working for Nortel. He caught the beginning of the telecommunications explosion. He would write technical and sales courseware as Nortel rolled out new innovations.

But after a year, there was a problem. Like most with the entrepreneurial spirit—even when it hasn't been fully realized—Jeff just didn't like working for a big company. He set out on his own, but Nortel liked him so much they offered him a contract to continue writing courseware.

The workload that Nortel provided was too much for one man, so he hired writers to help him write the courseware. The scope grew from just technical courseware to courseware on "training the trainers." And it just continued to grow.

Thus was born TelCom.

After a couple of years, US West came along and told him they needed help training 400 to 500 project managers, designers, and instructors. Jeff's company produced such impressive results that US West made Jeff's courseware their standard.

By the early 1990s, TelCom had revenues of $4 million and about forty full-time employees. Then Jeff's ship came in. Bell Canada wanted to outsource its corporate training program, and TelCom won the business. Almost overnight the company grew from 40 employees to 250. The contracts seemed to snowball as telecommunications deregulation spawned astronomical industry-wide growth.

Soon TelCom was doing all the optical training for Nortel. Then GTE (now Verizon) hired the company to figure out a way to outsource all of its training functions. For context, these are huge national and international companies dealing daily with high-tech, hard-learning curve issues, and training is an expense that ranks up among the highest costs to businesses, alongside payroll and real estate.

By the late 1990s, TelCom had seven North American offices generating revenues of $20 million. It was listed among the 100 fastest growing companies in Canada.

"At this point, we needed new capital to grow. We started talking to rollups that were looking for opportunities in telecommunications," Jeff said.

Rollups are venture capitalists or significant players in one industry who seek to put together several smaller companies in a fragmented industry to combine them into one big company. TelCom was courted by one: Advantage."

"I thought I was being cautious and made a deal with them where they could buy a third of the company each year over three years," Jeff said. "I figured that way I could get to know them, and as we completed the sale, to ensure that I and the company would be in good hands."

After months of negotiation and wrangling, TelCom and Advantage signed an agreement closing the deal. As part of the deal, TelCom was presented a check for $1 million.

As part of the buyout deal, half the value of the contract was to be paid in cash to TelCom shareholders, while the other half was to be paid in a set **number** of shares of Advantage stock—not, notably, in a set **dollar** amount of the company's stock. And that, it turns out, was a problem. Scant months after the deal closed, Advantage had a bad week. It was a doozy.

Advantage's CEO was in the midst of a divorce, and as part of the settlement he had to give his ex-wife half of his own stock in the company, which she sold. To market watchers, it looked like the CEO dumped half his stock in the company. The company also announced a $10 million restructuring. Then came news that it wouldn't meet its third quarter numbers. Likely the company's stock could have survived without much blemish any one of these events. But they all happened in the same week, and in that week Advantage's stock went from $26 per share to $13 per share.

Jeff recounts, "Well, I wanted out, and so I went back to them and told them so. There was no real recourse to me, so I had to settle for what they would offer, and fortunately our relationship with the founder was good enough that we were able to negotiate our way out. But they held the cards. To get out of the deal, I had to not only pay back the $1 million that was part of the initial deal, but another $500,000," Jeff said. "So my first acquisition cost me half a million bucks, going the wrong way."

LOST:

Half a million, cash.

WHAT HAPPENED:

HAVE AN OUT.

If you're playing the stock game—that is, if you're dealing with a public company in an acquisition relationship—you need to do extra due diligence. Jeff couldn't have forecasted the drop in stock, but for starters he should have known its numbers as well as its CEO knew his.

And while every contract is different, a critical difference for Jeff would have been if the sale was contingent not on a set amount of stock based on the price at signing, but in whole or at least in part a set dollar amount of the stock. Another solution is to have the buyer guarantee the price of the stock to be at minimum the share price at the date of sale.

SAME SONG, SECOND VERSE

So after selling his company—at a loss—Jeff was back in the driver's seat with business still going strong. Then along came Front Line, a rollup backed by a large venture capital fund out of Chicago, that was interested in acquiring TelCom.

"This time I said 'I'm getting half the cash up front,'" Jeff said. "The sale price was $11 million. We agreed to $6 million in private stock and $5 million in cash. They gave us $2.5 million of it up front, and the rest was to be delivered six months later, provided our company met certain numbers."

But, well, things didn't work out this time either. It turns out Front Line, which had been acquiring company after company, was increasingly seen by the venture capitalists as a money pit. Few of the companies it had acquired over the past couple of years were doing well, and the VC pulled back on its investment. Meanwhile, TelCom had met its numbers according to the contract and was eagerly awaiting a second check for $2.5 million.

"I'd assumed the money was in escrow or already set aside since they were signing the contract for it, and I hadn't specifically made that part of the contract," Jeff said. "I also failed to write in a penalty or forfeit clause if they failed to pay. Sure, they were in breach of contract, but since we'd be suing not just Front Line but also GE Capital, they could afford to keep us tied up in court indefinitely."

Jeff decided to cut his losses.

"At that point I realized I'd spent the last two-and-a-half years of my life selling the company, and I still had it," Jeff said, laughing at himself. "So I negotiated a deal with Front Line to sell my company again and split the proceeds with them."

Shortly thereafter, SmartForce—a $300 million a year public company—came along and Jeff sold TelCom to it, the deal done entirely in cash. The sale closed in June 2002, with Front Line going its way with its portion of the proceeds, and Jeff and SmartForce going their way together.

Or so it seemed.

A few months after the deal was closed, another company called SkillSoft came along to acquire SmartForce. And there was a slight problem, except it really wasn't Jeff's problem any more. SkillSoft didn't want TelCom's outsourcing service. Jeff was asked if he would buy the company back. After all, it would cost about $1 million alone just to shut the operation down, and Jeff had been paid $5 million for it—half of which went to Front Line to get untangled from it—so SkillSoft was going to lose money either way.

By this time, Jeff had had enough, and he wrote SkillSoft a terms sheet. He would offer it $1 for the company. What the hey—he didn't figure there were any other buyers, and it would save SkillSoft from having to spend the money to wind it down. For once, Jeff was in the catbird seat, calling the shots. But even though it looked like the deal might happen, SkillSoft found another buyer, and Jeff, after three years of selling the company and playing collections agent, was finally able to walk away.

Jeff is currently using the proceeds to work on developing his next venture. No entrepreneur can rest on his or her laurels for long. But he learned a lot in the journey that included starting a company he didn't really plan on, and then selling it not once, not twice, but three times.

LOST:

Over $3.5 million dollars and the opportunity to "move on to other things."

WHAT HAPPENED:

PROTECT YOURSELF.

"You have to ensure their stability even if they are ten times bigger than you are," Jeff says. "Be as careful with big companies as you are with little ones."

And remember: the deal is never done until the last dollar is in the bank.

"With Front Line, I gave away what I had, before it was paid for, and for lousy terms," Jeff says. "You don't give away what you have until it's paid for because you have to reconstruct it, as I did when the Front Line deal went south."

Include repercussions to failure in contracts. Penalties have to be that ownership reverts back as automatically as possible. Leases, signing authority, etc., will require the other company to sign off; if you don't have it built in to automatically revert, they can stall and delay indefinitely.

QUESTION:

Thinking of selling your business? If you don't want it back—and most people don't—have you left no stone unturned while researching your potential suitor? If taking any stock, have you protected yourself if it tanks?

TRENT VOIGHT

NAME: TRENT VOIGHT

COMPANY: PROCESS ENTERPRISES

INDUSTRY: CREDIT CARD PROCESSING

ANNUAL REVENUES: $5 MILLION

Some days you get the bear, and some days the bear gets you.

And sometimes your greatest challenges begin with your own mistake, but they take on an adversarial life of their own. This is one of those stories.

Trent Voight learned all this the hard way. A few innocuous and seemingly minor oversights on his part set up a situation where some people who claimed to be on his side tried to set him up for a fall—a sheep for the slaughter.

Problem was, though, they didn't count on the sheep turning himself into a sheepdog.

After working his way through computer engineering college at Baylor University, Trent went to work in Dallas for national convenience store holding company Southland Corporation. His first project was designing an automated system that sold events tickets using credit and ATM cards. As lead engineer on the Ticket Quick system, he quickly learned the world of credit card processing.

"I met my wife about that time—it was destiny because I met her at a nightclub when she was in town for one day for law school interviews, and I was out with my crew from Southland after working forty-eight hours straight on a project," Trent said. "Later when I started my own company, I realized how special our relationship was, because that's probably one of the hardest stresses you can put on a marriage. The hours are long, the money is not good—all the things that are tough on a marriage are compounded when you are doing a start-up."

The start-up that he proudly noted his marriage not only survived but thrived on was Process Enterprises. Established in 1990, it grew from a high-end point-of-sale development company to a credit card processing firm. By 1997, Process Enterprises had grown to the thirteenth largest company in the nation for credit card processing. It had about 30 employees and was doing $5 million in revenue.

In mid-1999, Trent was introduced to Vectrix Corporation, a rollup venture backed by a blue-chip investment firm. The rollup was to be a large e-commerce firm, and it needed a transaction processing company. Solid backers, an IPO pending, control of his own division, a generous acquisition offer—what wasn't to love?

Trent cut a deal where he'd be paid half the price in cash and the other half in stock, which was expected to skyrocket in value with the "pending" IPO. He would get half of the cash and stock up front, and the other half after he'd been with the company a full year. The deal closed in December, 1999, and for the first few months everything seemed to be going smoothly. Trent ran his division as he saw fit and the rest of Vectrix was growing, with more acquisitions.

However, there was a problem. (Does this sound familiar now?) Trent's division was successful. Too successful, it turns out. After a short while it looked as if the only division that was generating profits was Trent's transaction processing unit, and in hindsight Trent saw that the CEO was worried that power was moving in the wrong direction—away from the CEO and toward Trent.

"In hindsight, and this is not bragging—it's just a fact of where all the company's revenue was coming from—I was perceived as a distinct threat to the CEO. Plus, I have a Type A personality, so I don't cower well," Trent said. "So when they would say that we need to do this, and if I thought it was absolutely stupid, I would say 'That's absolutely stupid.' It doesn't endear you to some people when you are that blunt.

"For instance, they would do stuff like propose taking the customer information we had from these transactions we processed and sell the data to phone lists and marketing companies. Well, that will get you shut down in about an hour, and either they didn't know these basics or they didn't care," Trent said, his disdain for such practices still resonating as strongly as when he first heard of it. "This was people's privacy, and they wanted to stretch the rules or ignore them. I stopped them on proposals like that and I think that was a problem."

As this was unfolding, Trent had hired a marketing expert away from Discover Card® in Chicago to market his division. What he didn't know at the time was that the CEO and other senior management approached this marketing expert with a proposal to take over Trent's division.

What happened next was a sucker punch like few others.

"They held a management retreat because they were restructuring the company, and on Saturday morning they put up a slide that was the new orginaztion chart and my name was nowhere to be found on the chart!" Trent said. "It wasn't that I was fired; I was just not part of the organization. At that point I'm figuring I'm fired and they just haven't told me. In my place on the org chart was the marketing person I'd hired, who had as much business running the division as the man in the moon."

"They did everything in their power to move me into an office with nothing to do. I was told to do business development only and to have no decisions in transaction processing. In fact, multiple times I got yelled at because I tried to help the transaction processing division with problems," Trent said. "It was a total power play, and I finally realized what was going on."

Well, they wanted business development—so Trent went out and landed business. He signed a multimillion-dollar account with a client in San Francisco, but—and even Trent doesn't have an answer for exactly why—Vectrix just left it hanging.

For the most part, Trent just minded his own business after that—Vectrix's negligence of the account he'd signed left Trent personally with a black eye—and he proceeded to make plans for setting up his life after the year was out. But he wasn't entirely idle: He landed one more account for the transaction processing division with Bank of Omaha—set to begin the day after Thanksgiving, 2000, one of he busiest shopping days of the year. It produced almost 300,000 authorizations a week. Huge for the industry.

However, the first weekend after the account was set up, Trent got a call from Bank of Omaha saying that something was wrong—there was a mcrchant ID error. Trent checked it out, and sure enough there was a keying error—something rather common—that took about three minutes to fix. He was literally on his cell phone with the engineers in the time it took to correct the error.

"So ten days before my year was up, the CEO calls me in his office to fire me for 'negligence that harmed the company'— claiming it had harmed their relationship with Bank of Omaha," Trent said. "Which was crazy. What they thought was that they could get out of paying me the remainder of what they owed me for acquiring Process Enterprises."

Vectrix senior management thought they'd led the sheep to the slaughter. Problem was, Trent's transformation into sheepdog was already complete.

Everything he knew and did for the company lived on his laptop—which Vectrix owned. So he went out and bought an identical one and cloned it. He stuck the Vectrix laptop in his desk at their offices.

"So the day they fired me they told me to turn over my laptop. I told them it was in the drawer and what they found was a laptop with its operating system and that's about it. I had all my files and contacts and everything I needed to live on my own laptop, and I set up office the next day with a venture capital firm that I'd been working with anyway," Trent said. "They even wanted me to clean out my office that day and I told them 'No'. I had seen this coming and was more ready than they could have expected. I drove the show at the firing; they were really caught off guard. My attorney was already ready for something like this."

Aside from the usual felony and morals clauses, part of Trent's employment contract as part of the acquisition gave Vectrix the right to fire him for "acts injurious to the company"—something Trent subsequently realized was carte blanche.

So five months later, Trent and the Vectrix executives were in mediation. It was probably one of the quickest arbitrations on record. In the end, Trent got all his money, and in turn gave back the stock he had. Which suited him just fine.

"I knew the company was going downhill, so what I wanted was the cash," Trent said.

Months later, as he was awaiting the end of the twelve-month no-compete agreement and was making plans for setting up a new transaction processing company, Trent watched his old division's revenues at Vectrix fall by half. So he approached Vectrix and made an offer to buy back his own company.

Vectrix flat out said no.

So Trent carried on with his own plans, but then decided to try to reacquire the old company using a shell company as the buyer. Everything was going fine with the negotiations until the due diligence was underway. Trent was feeding questions to the shell company, and Vectrix realized the questions it had were too detailed for any outsider. So, knowing Trent was involved with the buyer, Vectrix backed out.

"That's when I realized that this was entirely personal," Trent said.

Oh, but that wasn't nearly the end. It gets better. And pettier. About eighteen months after Trent had been fired, Vectrix filed for bankruptcy. So Trent, still anxious to have his old company back, figured he would buy them out of bankruptcy.

"When it came time for them to allow potential bidders to do due diligence, they had financial reports in folders for every bidder—except me. My CFO went down there and they told her that she couldn't even use their copiers to make an extra report. But that was okay—she knew what to look for and I was with her on the phone the whole time," Trent said.

Had it sunk low enough? Not by far. In the end, the two interested and qualified bidders were Trent and a New York firm. On the day of the auction, Vectrix's attorneys objected to the judge that Trent was not a valid bidder on grounds that he didn't have a financial statement filed. Fortunately, Trent had one on him, and the judge and the creditors both agreed he was a viable bidder.

Trent won the auction on September 4, 2001.

Process Enterprises was his again, for twenty-eight cents on the dollar. It had only one customer left, but that didn't matter. Trent reassembled his old staff and took three months to get the company stable. By the seventh month, the company was breaking even. It was uphill from there, but the pace never slowed.

"We'll be back at $5 million revenue this year with good margins," Trent said. "This was a good business from the start. Just needed the right people and direction."

LOST:

$422,000 in legal fees and losses. Who knows how much, had the company never been bought by Vectrix.

WHAT HAPPENED:

LEAVE NO AMBIGUITY.

All employment contracts in acquisitions are designed to protect both parties, so there's always some give-and-take. But don't leave anything gray.

"I'll never agree in an employment contract to have anything held up again. I will let them have felony and morals clauses—the simple stuff, fine. But nothing generic. Nothing they can try to use to get out of paying me what is due," Trent says.

BIRD IN THE HAND?

If you are going to sell your baby—and there's no pat answer here—think long and hard. Either way it's a gamble. Trent says he would have taken more cash if he had it to do over again. The plans for an IPO never went into play, and the Vectrix management ended up running the company into the ground, along with the value of its stock.

MONEY TALKS.

Trent's company was only the second or third to be acquired by Vectrix, so there weren't really any prior-acquired company owners he could speak to about how they felt they were treated.

However, he believes in hindsight he could have talked to the individual investors. Several individuals had put between $50,000 and $100,000 into Vectrix.

"I probably should have talked to individual investors to see if they had a warm and fuzzy feeling. I found out after the fact that individual investors weren't entirely comfortable. They weren't getting good information, and that could have told me something," Trent says.

If you're going to be acquired, surely you want to know everything you can about who is doing the acquisition and who is pulling the strings.

QUESTION:

In an acquisition or merger, have you really done everything you can to protect your assets? Is there a Trojan horse lurking somewhere in the contracts you're signing? You've done your due diligence on the company you're dealing with—have you talked to other companies or investors it has dealt with before?

Have you made sure you have an avenue to receive all of your money in case your relationship with your buyer turns sour?

C O N C L U S I O N

"Nothing in the world can take the place of persistence. Talent will not; nothing is more common than unsuccessful men with talent. Genius will not; unrewarded genius is almost a proverb. Education alone will not; the world is full of educated derelicts. Persistence and determination alone are omnipotent.
■ *Calvin Coolidge*

The business leaders you've just read about were strapped onto nightmarish roller-coaster rides that went from the heights of success to the depths of despair—and, with persistence, back to the top once again. They share their stories not to gain sympathy but to give you the principles and tools required to not only survive in business but also to thrive. Their desire to give you these tools to succeed is far greater then the need to look good.

Fighting and ultimately surviving these devastating battles take a toll on a person's physical and emotional well being. How does one get through the tough times? After analyzing dozens of war stories, I determined that our ability to successfully bounce back depended on some universal ingredients that all business people should have in their lives.

First and foremost are options. They are NOT optional! Having options and choices in all areas of your life results in power, freedom, and peace. Mistakes happen when one is backed into a corner. Put your eggs in several baskets. That will result in maximizing your success and minimizing your stress.

Second, it is critical to surround yourself with loved ones who will act as a support system. Do you have a peer group off which you can bounce business ideas? So often we think we are all alone in dealing with the trials-and-tribulations of running a business. Not true. Groups exist all over the world that assist business owners, including Young Entrepreneurs' Organization (www.yeo.org), Young Presidents' Organization (www.ypo.org), The CEO Clubs (www.ceoclubs.org), The Executive Committee (www.teconline.com), and National Association of Women Business Owners (www.nawbo.org). Also find a mentor outside your peer group—a seasoned business executive, who is willing to share his or her wisdom and insight with you. Some of the above mentioned business organizations have mentor programs available to their members.

Living a healthy, well-balanced life also proves invaluable when dealing with prolonged stress. Stress has a serious negative effect on the brain's neurochemistry. What are the activities that can keep you moving, motivated, and give you an avenue to vent your frustrations? Running, tennis, fishing, golf, your favorite charity? People with healthy lifestyles and attitudes are more stress-resilient and are able to bounce back from adversity. I call my daily exercise routine "the drug of choice," because without it I doubt I would have survived my ordeal with my sanity intact.

I feel the most common mistake these entrepreneurs made was failing to do enough due diligence before putting their faith in a person or organization. When you take the time to research, analyze, and authenticate the information presented to you, your chances of failing will diminish significantly. Talk with someone who **wasn't** listed as a reference by the potential vendor or employee. Think outside the box—who can you speak to who can verify the validity of this person or company?

Another vital aspect that will guarantee success more than any other is PASSION. Expertise about a business or industry doesn't mean you care about it. A career should give your life meaning. It has been scientifically proven that having an emotional attachment to your business builds a stronger intellect, while drudgery actually weakens it. Being passionate about your business will allow you to persevere in ways you never thought possible.

Finally, play the game of business and life with authenticity, persistence, and integrity. Sometimes you will score the goal—and sometimes you will get scored upon—but at least you are not sitting on the sidelines! You are on the field, playing your heart out, gaining experience, wisdom, and success.

A B O U T   T H E   A U T H O R

 Carol Frank, MBA, is a former CPA who was bitten by the entrepreneurial bug. Having launched five successful companies, she is an expert on what entrepreneurs need to know to achieve and maintain success as well as how to avoid and overcome adversity in business. As such, she speaks to thousands of business leaders and entrepreneurs every year.

Do you have a unique and compelling story about successfully overcoming significant adversity? If so, we'd love it if you would send a two– or three–paragraph synopsis for possible inclusion on our website or in our next book.

CAROL FRANK AT 800-256-7265 EXT.10
CAROL@CAROLFRANK.COM,
OR VISIT WWW.CAROLFRANK.COM